WOOF DID YOU SAY?

EFFECTIVE TRAINING THROUGH COMMUNICATION AND UNDERSTANDING

B&H Bennett &
Hastings Publishing

ISBN #978-1-934733-08-0

DEDICATION

To my much loved family, both two-legged and four-legged. Also to all the dogs who are still neglected and misunderstood.

ACKNOWLEDGEMENTS

First for my family, who supported me and endured my near obsession with this project, the myriad of research books underfoot, and my scatterbrained attention to other aspects of life—especially towards the end as I became more and more absorbed with the project.

My parents, especially my father, who generously gave of their time and wisdom in helping me improve my writing style and ability to articulate my thoughts.

Martin Deeley, who encouraged me to hold to what was true and accurate, in spite of "political correctness". And for his great generosity in offering the Foreword to an otherwise unknown trainer. Thank You!

Brother Christopher Savage of the Monks of New Skete, for taking the time to review my manuscript and offer support and suggestions.

Randy Morrison, Electra-Eyed Productions, Robert Neary and Kevin Neary for their photos and illustrations.

Pat Andreason, Master Trainer, owner and President of Colorado Dog Academy, my former employer under whom I apprenticed years ago. Thank you for your skill and wisdom, and the ability to spark a drive for excellence in me. You are still considered the first truly adept trainer I had the pleasure to know.

My good friend, Valorie Putt, who never balked at taking time out of her busy schedule to answer my questions about computer skills and usage. Your patience will not be forgotten.

Celeste Bennett, whose skills allow even the "small fish" to have their voices heard.

And for all those wonderful students, both humans and canines, with whom it has been my great pleasure to work all these years. Your trust and support has helped me become a better trainer, teacher and, I hope, a better person.

Thank you all.

CONTENTS

FOREWORD

When I first entered the world of dogs and serious dog training, a few years back now, there was considerable emphasis on "making the dog do it". The dominant belief was that dogs did not want to work with their owners and had to be pressured into doing as required: that world was shaped by a very militaristic style of obedience training. I personally did not believe that was the only way, and I developed approaches based on my experience. That experience said that if a dog was trained correctly and a good relationship was built then the dog was willing to learn, wanted to lean and enjoyed the work. That said, there were, are and will be times when a dog willfully disobeys. My experience said that at those times we have to exert fair corrections to build good behavior.

In recent years there has been a move to remove any form of punishment and correction altogether. This philosophy advocates for training without correction; what some call a "totally positive" approach to training. Unfortunately, the books that have dwelt on this approach avoid many issues and behavioral problems that could be overcome with well-applied, fair corrections and punishment. On the few occasions I have heard "totally positive" practitioners deal with behavioral problems the solution has been theoretical rather than practical. More distressing has been the appearance of some "totally positive" practices that are actually corrections and punishment with some nice names and descriptions applied. That tends to mis-educate and lead to confusion over what practices are the most humane. Some followers of the "totally positive" philosophy condemn any trainer or owner who does not follow the dictates of their belief system; but the truth of the matter is *there are no ways to completely train a reliable dog without corrections that can include both rewards and punishment.*

What the realistic trainer/owner knows is that there is truth in both camps: "balanced reward/fair punishment" and "totally positive". Matching diverse learning and teaching methods to the personality, skills and natural abilities of your dog is an art. Learning itself is a complex process. Humans learn in diverse ways that include conceptual learning (through words and reason). Dogs learn through experience and consequences. They learn from us by association with situations and communications; through being shown, guided, led and molded.

At a time when most dog books are more intent on being politically correct, Stacey Neary comes across with a fresh breath of reality. She is unafraid to state and fully explain all approaches to training a dog. She describes how *humans* need to act and work in order to create a trusting relationship with their canine companions.

In this, her first book, Stacey uses a common sense approach that explains balance and understanding, gives practical how-to's and —most important of all—shows humane ways to bring up a great companion. In doing so Stacey does not shy from explaining the use of several approaches to learning. Her work describes the use of rewards, fair punishment and corrections to build a relationship and a companion that will be a lifelong friend.

This is training in equilibrium, a balanced and humane approach.

Martin Deeley, IACP CDT
UK Gundog Trainer of the Year 2007
Executive Director, Co-Founder IACP #1007

INTRODUCTION

Image courtesy Bennett & Hastings

Is love really blind? What do owners see when they look at their dogs? What do dogs see when they look back at us? As much as dogs are an integral part of the lives of many humans, as deep as the bond may go, it is still apparent that much of what drives the connection between owners and their dogs is generated largely by emotion and misunderstanding between the species. Assumptions about what motivates a dog, as well as anthropomorphizing our pets into four-legged humans still seems to drive a lot of the ways that owners deal with their dogs. The domestic dog, *Canis Lupus Familiaris*, has been living, working and coexisting on an intimate level with humans for tens of thousands of years. Maybe this long-term familiarity is what has caused us to forget that domestic dogs are still just a genetic stone's throw away from their relative, *Canis Lupus Lycaon*, the timber wolf. Intellectually I believe we are aware of this, but it rarely seems to effect how we think of our dogs on a day to day basis. How can that soft, cute, little Maltese, curled up at the end of the bed be the same as a 150-pound. wolf pursuing a caribou on the frozen tundra? Is love blind?

Dogs are primarily purchased for reasons of companionship. In so doing, owners naturally relate to their dogs as they would to another human or a child—wanting them to feel "part of the family". We offer love, affection and nurturing as a demonstration of our feelings for the dog. In essence, owners "humanize" dogs, treating them as furry little people. In those initial first weeks (and, indeed, the entire lifetime of the dog) we must not lose sight of the dog's close kinship with his wild cousin. While our dogs certainly enjoy and respond to our attentions, the *translated version* of our behavior into their canine language will likely mean something very different than what was originally intended. What the owners *thought* they were communicating to the dog may be a complete opposite from what the dog is "hearing".

The biggest problem in communication and training comes from two different species (dog and man) trying to use their own individual languages in the process. Dog language is different from human language in many very important ways. Owners may understand this in theory but in practice it is often hopelessly "lost in translation". Dog and owner alike can often get frustrated through an unproductive relationship where both parties are confused because of an inability to communicate their needs or wishes. Oftentimes owners simply give up or just run out of steam and momentum trying to teach good behavior to their dogs.

As the drive to be humane to dogs has grown, in some cases it has "taken over" the training process,

even to the point of pushing common sense out the door. Fortunately, humane treatment and common sense are *not* incompatible, and can walk side-by-side in the training process. Understanding the dog's drives, his perspective and how he views his world should determine the training approach. It should be flexible enough to meet and satisfy these same drives and perspectives. There are many different approaches to training, some more effective than others. The purpose of this book is not to condemn methods that aren't identical to the ones laid out within these pages, but rather to present a "canine-oriented" approach that seems to fit with the dog's view of the world. A sizeable segment of my clientele is made up of group class "rejects"— those who were kicked out of, or failed group classes, or those who felt there must be another way than the "biscuit route". My business has grown steadily over many years because my methods produce positive results. Both the dogs and their owners are content, educated and have a deeper appreciation for one another when they are done—*and* they are understanding each other's language. In an attempt to remain true to my philosophy and methods, this book is meant to educate and train *people who handle dogs* more than the dogs. Over the years I've learned that the simple daily dynamic between dog and owner can, and usually does, have a profound impact on a dog's responsiveness to instruction. Understanding how the dog *perceives* you and your actions is a large part of the "human" training process, getting the dog's attention, and earning his respect.

Good quality training is not aimed at crushing the dog's spirit. On the contrary, it should demonstrate an awareness of the dog's potential—both good and bad. It should show a pro-active and educated mind-set, wanting the best for the dog, yourself, and the people around you. "Genuine training is about freedom— freedom for both ourselves and our dogs to enjoy each other, enhancing our relationships by allowing their potential to blossom in the patient context of trial and error, praise and appreciation."[1]

More than 20 years ago, when dogs entered my life as an adult I had the overly confident, naïve notion that "I would teach them". As the years have passed though, I have to say that quite the opposite has occurred. As each dog has entered my life, whether as a student or one of my own, I have been given another chance to glimpse life through their eyes. Each dog has had something unique and different to offer and teach *me*. In the end, I have to say that I have been more *their* student than the other way around.

What I have learned from them is covered in this book—a handling of their language and method of communication. Incorporating behaviors that dogs use among themselves, I have combined training and dog psychology in an attempt to help you better understand your dog and thus achieve a bond that goes far beyond the reach of a leash. In our quest to have "better dogs", we must learn to be better humans.

[1] *I & Dog*, The Monks of New Skete. Yorkville Press, New York, New York. 2003. pg. 21

· FELIX ·

Photography: Kevin Neary

CHAPTER 1
NATURE VS. NURTURE

▪ A DOG'S-EYE VIEW OF THE WORLD ▪

How we adore our dogs. We literally dote on them. We buy them the most colorful toys, the funniest little squeakies, the softest, plushest beds. We seek out the highest rated healthy dog food and the yummiest treats. We take them to the park and arrange "play dates" for them. We relinquish our sofas and often even share our beds with them. So **why** do they seemingly ignore us and refuse to come or stay or heel? You'd think all that adoration from us would be worth something to our canine friends. Then why does it seem so difficult to get them to pay attention? Is there something wrong with the dog? Or is the problem with us? What is it that we are communicating to our dogs, through our actions, that is a stumbling block to obedience?

The fault, if any, exists in attempting to change the nature of the dog to fit our human needs or expectations. We like to ascribe human characteristics to our dogs, using "human" emotions and feelings to make sense out of their behavior. We seem to enjoy making the claim that our dogs "think they're people". Nothing could be further from the truth. Dogs do not have the ability to be anything other than what they are—a dog. Ascribing human attributes to dogs and trying to relate to them on a "human" level

is to ignore their own unique qualities. Further, it can only distort and reduce effectiveness when it comes to training. Dogs are no more human than humans are dogs. To truly understand your animal, start trying to view the world from her perspective.

It's all too common for humans to attempt communicating with their dogs using our own language system. Gestures that, to us, are meant to display friendliness and openness, often translate poorly to the dog. Not understanding their perspective or view can lead to confusion or worse, tragedy. Just as importantly, signals that dogs send us are often misinterpreted, again producing problems and frustration. Dogs lack the capabilities to speak, and their "reasoning" abilities are subject for debate. Rather, communication between dogs is achieved through the subtleties of body language, visual cues and energy. They are more aware of the slight changes in our posturing and expressions than we are. If you truly wish to understand your dog, start by looking critically at the way *your actions appear to her.*

As humans, people have an ability and desire to love and nurture. That's one of the main reasons we like pets. We direct all this emotion and attention on our dogs, somehow, (and I believe quite unconsciously) hoping they'll be grateful and obedient in return. Without actually being aware of it, owners are trying to buy respect with affection and, in some cases, leniency. Unfortunately, affection and obedience are two completely separate issues to a dog. Any given day of the week, it's possible to see a dozen examples to support this. Face it—if loving a dog was all that was required to make her obey, there would probably be a lot more well-behaved dogs. The truth is that while affection has an important and prominent place in obedience and in the dog/human relationship, one does not produce the other. I repeat, affection alone does not generate obedience.

In the truest sense, love for another being does not simply imply a warm, fuzzy feeling, prompting us to buy candy, flowers, or, in the case of a dog, plush toys and chew bones. It should involve looking at the totality of this being and appreciating its uniqueness and individuality. Love translates into a more dynamic relational rapport that also addresses the needs of this "other party" and the desire to bring out the best in them. Looked at in this light, there is a spirituality in connecting with your dog, one that will humble and hopefully encourage you to move beyond the limited human perspective. In *How To Be Your Dog's Best Friend*, the Monks of New Skete state that because "dogs are guileless... they don't deceive. When we take seriously the words they speak to us about ourselves, we stand face-to-face with the truth of the matter." When we pay attention to "these words... inscribed on their bodies, in their expressions, in the way they approach and interact with us,"[1] they can stimulate a new level of consciousness.

[1]*How To Be Your Dog's Best Friend,* The Monks of New Skete. Little, Brown and Company, New York. 2nd Ed. 2002, pg. 8

Training a dog should be looked at as a total education process (for both owner and dog) rather than simply teaching what a few words mean in association with some random body movements. Commands can easily be taught in just a few short weeks. On the other hand, raising a dog who is respectful, calm, content and a joy to have around is a life-long pursuit. We send our children to school not simply to learn to tighten nuts and bolts on an assembly line. We send them to school to learn an awareness of others, to have a broader view of the world, and to develop a respectful outlook on life. Such should also be the goal when we look at training our dogs.

All too often, the concept of dog training is seen as a remedy to certain isolated issues, i.e. teach the dog not to do this, that or the other thing. We want to use it as a solution to an immediate problem, rather than looking at a "big picture". We want to guide the dog to repeat only certain behaviors and not others. But most of these ideas stem from the premise that, first and foremost, regardless of what *we're* doing, the dog's behavior must change. It lays little to no responsibility at *our* feet. The most effective trainers realize that the majority of problems arising between dog and handler are not inherently the fault of the dog—rather, they're the fault of the person holding the leash. To a great extent, the dog simply behaves in a natural way as a *response* to the messages and energy you send him. To deal individually with each little annoying behavior (i.e. digging, barking, jumping, running away) can too easily deny a larger picture. Specific behaviors are more accurately seen as indicators of the overall relationship you have with your dog, and whether or not all the needs of the dog are being satisfied, both physical and psychological. Thus, behavioral displays reveal the roles that the dog (and you) are playing in the daily dynamic. You might likely be more of the flaw in the communication process than he is.

When people think of dog training, visions of a group class often appear, where all dogs are enthusiastically motivated and focused while the handler's pockets bulge with treats. This is a very popular approach to training and can help some people quite a bit, a moderate amount of people to a small degree, and a lot of people not at all. What is often lacking with these methods is any explanation or implementation of true dog psychology. The most effective programs must, by definition, build off the dog's inherent nature. You wouldn't, for example purchase a strawberry plant and then expect it to produce figs. And yet, in a way, we often expect unreasonable things from our dogs. Comments such as "He *knows* he's not supposed to do that…" reveal an underlying assumption that dogs can somehow deduce our wishes without any clear communication. What actually generates "obedience" from a dog is something completely different than what one might expect.

▪ How Dogs Learn ▪

In the study of dog behavior, two distinct categories are recognized. First, there are behaviors that need no teaching, i.e. genetically programmed behavior, such as the hunt-drive or reproduction. Second, there are those behaviors (primarily social) that the dog must learn. A dog is not born knowing innately how to interact appropriately with others. He learns that through social contact, first and foremost from his mother and then from his siblings. Within a pack, as the pup grows, other adults also assist in teaching the youngster what is accepted and where he fits in. This is the beginning of the social structure within a pack. A dog doesn't inherently know what is expected of him—you must teach him and make it clear through your behavior and responses.

It is generally accepted that the use of methods called "operant conditioning" are the most effective when it comes to training of dogs. These philosophies and methods go back to behavioral researchers such as C. Lloyd Morgan and Konrad Lorenz (pioneering ethologists) and more recently by B.F. Skinner. All deal with the learning process that involves reinforcement (some positive and some negative) for certain behaviors. When social interaction is observed within a pack setting, there is an even balance between success and failure, the pup thus learning rules and the acceptable boundaries for social behavior. When it comes to training dogs, many human versions of this process place an excessive amount of attention on the "positive" reinforcement, with the "negative" reinforcement being down-played, even out-and-out avoided with some programs. This goes against the way that a dog will learn, left to his own devices.

Dogs learn what works and what doesn't by the process of *trial and error*. This includes the existence of consequences, positive and negative, for a particular behavior. If one behavior is tolerated or *rewarded*, or if the dog sees some benefit to the action, it will be repeated. This aspect of the dog's learning process is primarily what "positive training" capitalizes on. This, in and of itself, is not wholly ineffective. However, there is another part to the learning process that is equally important in helping the dog develop good judgment. It is the part about how she learns through *non-successful behaviors*. A dog will generally *not* repeat a behavior for which she sees no tangible gain, *or a behavior that is met rapidly with a negative consequence*.

One Montana winter, my parents' English Springer Spaniel, Hobbes, was doing what came naturally to his breed, chasing birds. Unfortunately, this particular day, the birds happened to be a flock of geese that had landed on the ice on the lake in front of their house. In a frenzy of delight and instinct, Hobbes took off across the snow, then the ice, and then, before he knew it, had fallen through the ice. (Relax, this story doesn't end in tragedy.) It took him a couple minutes before he was able to get to a patch of ice that afforded him some traction to pull himself out. As he got off the lake, he was quickly grabbed up by my parents and brought inside to thaw out. The point of this story is that Hobbes *learned* through that incident to stay off the ice, and even leave geese alone (other birds are still fair game). He never approaches the edge of the lake

anymore in winter. One might have been able to work for weeks or months to *condition* the dog to stay off the ice or leave geese alone, but it would never have the impact of *learning* it first-hand through a negative consequence. This demonstrates the whole difference between purely "positive" conditioning only, as opposed to allowing a dog to "learn" through some degree of negative consequences. While I don't wish at all that dogs would have to learn through life-threatening situations, the point is that the owner should carry this responsibility seriously, looking out for the dog and using *controlled* negatives as well, to help him learn.

Leon F. Whitney, in *Dog Psychology, the Basis of Dog Training*, states that conditioned reflexes can be achieved by corrections as well as rewards, but "that the *two can be used together most effectively*"[2] (emphasis added). When it comes to training, eliminating corrections is as unreasonable as eliminating rewards. One would never dream of removing rewards from the process. And yet trainers who support using an occasional correction have certainly gotten a "black eye" over the last generation or so. Perhaps this desire to eliminate any "confrontation" goes back to that "warm, fuzzy" feeling again. But how fair is this really to the dog? It serves little purpose if the training methods distort the underlying message — human leadership, to the point that it becomes unrecognizable. Overcompensation with one aspect of training doesn't make up for the nonexistence of the other.

[2]*Dog Psychology, The Basis of Dog Training*, Leon F. Whitney, D.V.M. Howell Book House, Inc. New York. 12th Ed. 1984, pg. 121

Thus, *how* you teach your dog should be as critical as *what* you teach your dog. Keeping the reinforcements balanced (both positive and negative) should be an important issue when exploring training philosophies and implementing training methods. The specific and deliberate avoidance of any corrections when training seems to be gaining in popularity. Many trainers adhere to it and claim great success. Avoiding the use of coercion and the concept of having to "correct" a dog is pleasing to many people. It seems to fit in with a new "enlightened" view of the world around us. But how does this sit with a dog? Does he *really* understand the whole purpose of *why* you're behaving in such a manner? Does he grasp that you want to be the leader in between all those biscuits? Is that truly the way his mind is wired? Just because you want to be enlightened in your approach doesn't mean the dog is thinking the same way. At some point it seems appropriate to step back from the picture and examine how the dog might actually be translating our actions and what they mean to him. While a thoughtful and educated approach to training should indeed include more positive reinforcement than negative, attempting to avoid corrections altogether denies that a dog can successfully learn from both—and *not* be psychologically scarred from the experience. (Remember Hobbes on the ice?) Even Karen Pryor, a staunch supporter of positive training, in her book *Don't Shoot the Dog*, outlines eight possible methods for changing undesirable behavior (some of which use aversives) and herself admits that "each (of the eight approaches) has its place"[3]

[3] *Don't Shoot The Dog*, Karen Pryor. Bantam Books, New York. 1985. pg 99

Humans typically translate "positive reinforcement" into the concept of "reward", hence it becomes something tangible—something we can hand out. Roger Abrantes states that "Reward is usually defined as a pleasant thing that the individual experiences after performing a certain action. However, using this example, the use of a reward as reinforcement is mistaken, as it has no *learning* effect at all."[4] (emphasis added). This implies there is an intrinsic difference between *learning* and simple *conditioning*. The strongest training methods should use some of both.

Training methods that attempt to avoid the issue of "error" prevent the dog from learning and growing in a three dimensional world, or from developing an ability to make a choice based on experience, knowledge and awareness. They also leave the trainer with the heavy burden of having to make sure the "positive" reinforcement is so fantastic that the dog will always choose it over any other potential distraction. But refusing to allow for failure in a natural way invariably lends itself to some potentially counterproductive consequences in the overall results.

First, there is the tendency to exaggerate the *intensity* of the positive reinforcement. As mentioned above, this often happens because a dog can get bored with the reward after a time—even following a regime of what is called an "intermittent schedule of

---

[4] *Dog Language, An Encyclopedia of Canine Behaviour.* Roger Abrantes. Wakan Tanka Publishers. 1997. Distributed by DogWise. Wenatchee, WA. pg. 211

rewards"; randomly dispensing rewards. It's the old, "bigger, louder, flashier" syndrome. Not only is too much emphasis placed on the success of the dog, but also on the *degree* of success. In other words, if telling the dog he did a good job is appropriate, then why not send him to the moon with your praise? Why not keep him in a constant state of anticipation and glee throughout the training process? Why not use a motivational device that keeps him on the edge of his seat? Relying excessively on the "reward" all too easily lends itself to overdoing it on the intensity, producing an animal who's too wound up with anticipation for her own good. No law says the positive reinforcement must be a treat or an annoying squeak toy. Sometimes, a dog might just as easily be content with a good scratch on the ears, a belly rub, a kind look or a soothing voice. And she will probably be calmer as a result.

During an initial consultation once, I observed one of the most hyperactive Golden Retrievers I'd ever seen. Obviously, one of the behaviors the owners wanted to address was the dog's constant state of seeming hyperactivity. He ran around, back and forth, up and down, grabbing toys and panting like a freight train the entire visit. The dog couldn't have been enjoying himself. He had to have been absolutely exhausted by the time I left—and it was all self-imposed. The problem was that this dog was in a constant state of anticipation. Many months ago, during his original training, the dog had been given treats for every little thing he did. Thus, he grew into a state of perpetual expectancy, wondering when the next reward would come his way. The unbalanced

nature of the original training was painfully obvious with this dog. The solution was to completely eliminate food from the process, substituting verbal and physical praise. Within a few weeks, the frenetic behavior was significantly improved.

Another example involving excessive use of food rewards involved a couple with a Springer Spaniel mix. They contacted me regarding issues over food guarding aggression. Their 8-month old female had apparently always displayed growling during meals, and been particularly temperamental with edible chews and biscuits. Nevertheless, the methods they were told to employ with the initial training were all about food rewards, severely exacerbating this particular dog's tendencies. By the time they contacted me, the growling had spilled over into other areas — when they were simply petting the dog, or just walking past her bed.

These examples do not imply that all dogs will become this hyperactive or aggressive as a result of overemphasizing rewards. It simply shows how these approaches might exacerbate a pre-existing tendency in a dog.

Second, over-emphasizing rewards too often confuses "commands" with "tricks". A *trick* is fun for both dog and handler, but serves no essential purpose, except for amusement. A *command*, on the other hand, is not taught for the sake of amusement, nor should it be considered optional. It should be synonymous with the word *rule*. I have worked with countless dogs who knew what a word meant, but had no notion of it being a command or a "social expectation". In the dog's view, the choice of whether to respond or not was purely discretionary, based on the presence or absence of a favored "reward". The idea is, at some point, to wean the dog off the treats or the toy. Unfortunately, in practice, a lot of owners just continue with the reward (it's so easy, after all) not realizing what this is doing to the dog's perspective and the relationship as a whole.

A good example of this happened many years ago. The dog's owners assured me their pooch understood the word "Down". Several unsuccessful attempts were made to get the dog into the "Down" position. Each time the command was given the dog looked up with curious anticipation but would not cooperate. It was at this point that the owners informed me they always gave the dog a treat for this. I encouraged them to demonstrate. Comically, as the owner left to get the dog treats, inadvertently shaking the box in the process, back in the front room the dog has suddenly decided to lie down. All it took was the *sound* of the treats to get the desired response. While this actually was rather humorous, it serves as a good demonstration of the issue of "trick" vs. "command" in the debate over the reward system. Who was training whom?

Third, relying solely on positive reinforcement tends to avoid or ignore the issue of mistakes. Training methods that adhere rigidly to Skinner's learning theory are, by admission, based on rules of *probability*,

not absolutes. Only supplying owners with the means to "reward" a dog leaves them ultimately ill-prepared and possibly ill-served when the "laws of probability" run short. In real-life, dogs respond to their environment. They can (and often do) act on that same environment as well. Every dog considers briefly, at least some of the time, whether or not to respond to a command. The reasons why dogs choose not to respond are varied, but suffice it to say that it comes with the territory. For the sake of safety (for both dog and human) and realism, trainers should be obligated to supply owners with *all* the "tools" that might be needed to train and keep their dogs safe. Leashes and training collars are not detrimental to the learning process, especially when owners are taught humane and effective use of these tools.

While an approach that emphasizes rewards may enhance certain types of training (i.e. search and rescue, agility, field competition, etc.) it simply misses the primary motivation for obedience. Enhancing the dog's instinctive drives may be appropriate for the aforementioned disciplines. Obedience, however, is supposed to get in touch with the psychology of the pack. According to Roger Abrantes in *Dog Language, An Encyclopedia of Canine Behavior,* "The social individual's task was: 'to fulfill my will, without killing or harming the other, *who I need for my survival* and that of my offspring'"[5] (emphasis added). Further, he states that dogs are one of the creatures, along with humans, who are "masters of compromise". The dog actually understands and accepts the benefits of

[5]*ibid* pg. 211.

pack structure—give and take. The dog understands his very survival may depend on the strength and disciplined nature of the pack. A pack that operates as a team is more likely to survive. This fact about the social nature of dogs is well-established and supported through decades of research and study. With obedience, the goal is to simulate that pack social structure. Hence, the motivation is different. The establishment of rules and expectations is *not* just entertainment to the dog.

With this in mind, then, finally and most importantly, training methods that use solely positive reinforcers fail to address a critical aspect of the dog's perspective: *"Who is in charge?"* Regardless of whether an owner wants to address it, this *is* an important part of the dog's psyche. Dogs do not operate on the paradigm of a utopian paradise where all creatures have equal say in the governing process. Someone must be in charge! This is not in any way to imply that everything a dog does can be explained or lumped into a neat category of "dominance and submission". The dynamic between **conspecifics** (fellow species members, usually of the same pack) is varied and intricate, involving many levels of interaction. However, quite simply stated, leaders within a pack are those animals that *establish and enforce the rules, and control the resources.* This is done in a variety of ways, often creatively, depending on the situation and the specific dog. I have had many a human student tell me "I don't care if the dog sees me as the leader, as long as he pays attention." This statement is more revealing of the *human* perspective

than it is of the dog's. However, if the training process *can* address this aspect of the dog's psychological make-up, it will have been all the more successful. By the same token, training that ignores the dog's search for structure and a leader, dismisses a critical part of his predisposition as unimportant or even non-existent.

Social by his very make-up, he is "wired" for leadership. Without structure and a leader, he is lost. Studies done on dogs in the wild demonstrate how quickly a pack can fall apart if the alpha is killed. Every dog wants to know what the rules are. That's how he determines his identity within the pack. Without understandable, primal communication, dogs flounder, attempting to establish order and rules out of thin air. When we observe mother teaching her pups during the first few weeks of life, we observe what might seem to us to be strong moves on Mom's part. These might include growling, nipping, or even pinning the pup to the ground. Mom knows that the pups' survival may depend on their acknowledgement of her authority and their ability to pay attention. When observing "Mom's" method, though, the interesting fact to focus on is that *the pup learns* and no real harm is done to him.

The focus of this book, then, is to examine the *entire relationship* and training process from the dog's perspective. A lot of times this requires a close look at ourselves as well. When working with dogs, it is of the utmost importance to be disciplined and aware of *yourself.* Bringing emotional "baggage", or intellectual limitations to the training table can only hamper your effectiveness in connecting with the dog. If a dog isn't performing well, it's not unreasonable to look at the one holding the leash first. Everything you're feeling can be detected through the leash! One might argue that we want the best for and from our dog. In fairness, though, he deserves the same from you.

Once while observing a student of mine working on the Heeling exercise, I wasn't surprised that the dog's performance and attentiveness deteriorated rapidly every time the owner responded to a call on her cell phone. I tactfully suggested she leave the phone at home when walking with the dog, explaining that the two of them deserved this time to focus just on each other. Not surprisingly, *sans* cell phone, both participants seemed to benefit and improve on their attentiveness. Some students have even confessed to me in moments of great honesty, that working with their dogs has made them aware of their deepest personality characteristics—not all of which made them proud. It's hard to hide behind a leash.

Why we do what we do with dogs can be very revealing. But why we *avoid* doing certain things can be just as revealing. Is the overall relationship and rapport balanced on both sides, or does the owner side-step certain aspects of training and instruction because of his or her own personal views or limitations? These are hard questions, but should be addressed before picking up the leash. There is much more to training a dog than "textbook philosophy", technique and timing.

Appreciating the learning process from the eyes of the other participant is critical to establishing the best rapport possible. As stated earlier, the dog is unable to appreciate our perspective. In that sense, we definitely have the advantage in being able to place ourselves in his "paws". Allowing your dog to actually teach you a few things will deepen the relationship and level of understanding. Balanced companionship should allow room for the blossoming of both participants.

▪ First Things First: Fido's "Pyramid" ▪

Before beginning the discussion of the "how" of dog communication, discussing *priorities* seems to be appropriate. In the process of training and communication, these are critical. Humans and dogs both have priorities. Surprisingly, they are not that different. Similar to "Maslow's Hierarchy of Needs", the needs at the bottom of the pyramid take up most of the space, the priorities above those building on the solidity of those below. To produce a physically and psychologically balanced animal, and to maximize the effectiveness of training, a dog must have certain needs met—and in a particular order. Putting the dog's priorities in proper order demonstrates an awareness of how a healthy relationship is based on mutuality. Making a commitment to do this is well worth the effort.

▪ Physical Needs ▪

At the base of the pyramid are the physical needs. This means food, water, shelter and *exercise*!

Too many dogs in urban settings don't get the exercise they need. All dogs, from 2-pounds to 200-pounds need regular exercise. As an animal, this is critical to physical and mental health. If a dog is always tense due to pent up energy, she can't pay attention in "school". Especially with a young or highly active dog, this would be like a kindergartener kept for a 7-hour school day with no recess. Canine obesity (very common in this country) is one of the worries with sedentary lifestyles. But there are also other long term effects of unreleased energy. Sometimes they can internalize, manifesting themselves in obsessive-compulsive behaviors or even self-mutilation.

What type of exercise a dog receives is critical. Be prepared to be *personally* involved in this aspect of the dog's development. When I ask students how often they exercise their dogs, the answer is sometimes "not too often, but we have a backyard". This is not the solution to this issue. Just because a dog has access to a backyard doesn't mean she is getting the exercise she needs. Even if she does run around a bit, it won't be on a sustained basis, providing her with a serious "work-out". *You* need to give that to her. And, by the way, roughhousing, play-fighting and chase games *are not* considered reasonable exercises. Read more on that in Chapters 2 and 3. The best forms of physical release should be controlled, *structured,* and of a continuous nature. In a pinch, a solid game of fetch can work if the dog plays according to the rules (i.e. no chase games or tug-of-war). But, hands-down the best exercise for the dog is long,

daily, brisk walks—no matter how short the legs (yours or the dog's). The finer points of Heeling are covered in Chapters 5 and 6. Remember, there is a message sent in every interaction, mainly in the *how* of the activity. Walks, specifically *Heeling*, are exercise with structure, guidance and leadership!

Many working breeds benefit greatly from doing what they were actually bred for—it comes naturally. Consider options such as herding, field training (i.e. hunting) agility or obstacle courses. Fly-ball groups seem to be very popular with certain breeds as well. Even tracking and trailing are worth looking into for scent hounds. These activities are fairly prevalent and can be accessed through the internet for local groups in your area.

The important point to all these suggested activities are that they involve *two* types of exercise—physical *as well as* mental. The dog is *thinking* as he is exercising. And, as common sense would guess, the positive benefit to a consistent exercise regimen is that *tired dogs are far less mischievous.*

• Psychological Needs •

Taking care of the dog's exercise and physical needs is about half the battle. If that's all the owner addresses, however, the dog's *mental* energy is still left to play havoc. Strive for balance at both ends—body *and* mind. Ignoring the fact that the dog needs mental stimulation as well can produce something like the "all brawn and no brains" syndrome. Some years back, a single woman with an adolescent German Short-Haired Pointer called for assistance in calming her dog down. She was worn out from trying to "wear him out". She said that she diligently walked him every day, even upwards of 6 miles in length (she was putting *me* to shame). For awhile, she said, it seemed to do the trick. But now, she and the dog were both in such incredibly good shape that it no longer seemed to calm him down as it had in the past. The problem was that she had quite dramatically neglected his *mental and psychological* needs. She had channeled only *half* of his energy, leaving the mind to go to seed.

Mental energy in dogs is very real, even though we may have a hard time noticing it. The more specialized the breed, the more acutely the mind needs to be stimulated. Bird dogs, herding dogs and many terrier breeds need a lot of mental gymnastics to keep them calm and content. Do not ignore this aspect of the dog's needs. It can make all the difference in the world keeping them happy and pleasant to live with.

Under this category, we have the concept of *companionship and rules*. Introducing a dog to a new home, usually involves a 7-10 day adjustment period, during which a dog becomes acclimated to the new surroundings. During this time he will become familiar with his new home and do some preliminary bonding with new "pack members". In spite of the challenges associated with house-training, the dog should be allowed access to the inside of the house as much as possible.

As a social creature, his need to have contact with others and to feel part of a group is a big part of balanced psychological development. Isolating a dog in a back yard or a dog run for the majority of his existence produces a bored and lonely animal. His limited interaction with the rest of the pack only serves to psychologically frustrate him. For many dogs, constant isolation is mental torture. It typically creates an animal who sees himself as the shunned "omega" dog, but he never really understands why. Training dogs like these can often be difficult because it takes so long to calm them down. Part of what produces exceptional results in training is the depth of the dog-human bond in the relationship. Connecting with your dog should go beyond a few minutes here and there throughout the day. It also involves using your *physical presence* to help satisfy his need for companionship. The more the dog is allowed into the human's space and the human's life -style, the deeper the bond will grow, as well as his willingness to cooperate.

Once the dog has transitioned into feeling part of the new group (i.e. companionship needs are met) his next move will be to begin figuring out the social structure — what his place is and how he fits in with the other pack members. He needs, and is looking for, *rules*. This is how each animal learns what his function is. This hierarchy is a pre-established structure wherein each dog has a role and purpose. Believe it or not, the very games you might be playing with your dog are part of this process. I refer to them as "passive messages". He's using *your* behavior to determine his ranking and the existence or nonexistence of rules. In the natural environment, rules are imposed on puppies by higher ranking members. Specifically, that would be the mother, higher ranking adults, and/or (in a pack of wolves) the alpha male and female.

Later in this book, there will be more detail on *how* dogs establish social structure, but for now, it is important to understand that the construction of this social order will begin after the first week—sometimes even sooner. In other words, the *dog* will begin construction, possibly without the owner even being aware of it. The dog starts reading and reacting to the human's behavior as a way of figuring out her pack rank. Are you fair, firm and consistent? Are you ambivalent and confused? Do you behave in a calm and dignified manner? Or are you constantly playful and rambunctious with her? Do you hand out treats left and right? Do you praise your dog calmly with your touch, eyes and voice? Do you usually give in to her demands for attention, or do you sometimes make her "wait"? Your dog learns to "read" you, and responds accordingly.

In the dog world, communication is achieved through posturing, eyes, facial expressions, vocalization, gesturing and sometimes even snapping and biting. These displays are no "game" to the dog. They are his language, the only one he knows. You'll need to learn it too, for in order to be the pack leader, you must be fair and understandable.

With dog communication and interaction, there are relatively few benign activities. Nearly everything an owner does with their dog; how they do it, the touch, the voice, the level of attention given to the dog and for what reason, sends messages to him. The dog processes all of it in an attempt to figure out his place in the pack. Constructive interaction using leader-like behavior and dog psychology produces a calm, respectful animal who follows you willingly. Rambunctious, playful interaction, rough play or excessive coddling and fawning over a pup or dog produces just as easily the reverse—a demanding, spoiled animal who is anything but obedient, especially when you really need it.

The reason is fairly simple. To the dog, she's been receiving "mixed messages". Trying to play both roles (leader and playmate) in the relationship with a dog serves only to confuse her. In short, one is either the leader, or not. Engaging in deliberately contentious play where you appear to be the dog's equal one minute, and then in the next, suddenly switching gears and putting on the "supervisor's cap" is too confusing and too ambiguous for the dog. You can't "have your cake and eat it too"—at least not at the *developmental stage* of the relationship and the training. A few mixed messages in the beginning are not usually serious. If a dog is sassy and uncooperative on Tuesday, it doesn't mean that by Wednesday, he'll be wearing the royal diadem. Dog's don't lie awake at night thinking about how to overthrow the social structure. However, the accumulation of mixed signals over a prolonged period will most definitely affect his view of the relationship and his willingness to follow your lead.

Consistency in handling and in your behavior is critical. Any good trainer or dog behaviorist will agree with the consistency of *dog* behavior. Dogs are not unpredictable. The truth is, it's usually the humans in the equation who bring inconsistencies into the relationship. Learn from your dog and strive to give her a balanced, predictable life. You'll both appreciate the benefits.

■ Start Early If Possible ■

One of the primary goals with my students is encouraging them to begin training with their puppies as soon as possible. As mentioned earlier, one week of adjustment is really all that's needed before it's reasonable to begin building a social structure with the dog. A pro-active approach models after a mother dog. Mom guides and teaches her pups as soon as they are mobile and their eyes open. While instruction is gentle to start—amounting to not much more than a nudge—it is nevertheless going on. The reprimands from Mom tend to get gradually sterner and more demonstrative as the pups get bigger and more rambunctious. The point, though, is that training starts early.

Most people equate one year of a dog's life to about seven years for a human. This may be a little off, but for the sake of this model let's say it's accurate. If so, then waiting until a dog is 6 months of age or older to begin his formal training would be comparable to allowing a child to be free of guidance or

instruction until the ripe old age of 3½. You'd likely have a holy terror on your hands! A dog's brain develops rapidly, being primarily complete by about 6 weeks of age. Getting in touch with your dog's mind early and guiding him down the correct paths will make all the difference in the world later in his life.

This is not to imply that older dogs cannot be trained. Theoretically, it's never too late to change an unproductive relationship. Don't underestimate your dog's ability or willingness to move forward. But the fact remains that it is easier to establish good habits in the beginning than to have to correct and change bad ones down the road.

Puppy training doesn't have to be arduous or exhausting. A few minutes at a time, a few times a day can produce a profound change in his behavior and attitude. The idea is to get him used to the existence of rules from the very beginning. A dog that grows up with this as part of his point of reference is a more content and more manageable animal—no matter what stage of his life.

CHAPTER 2

WELCOMING THE NEW PACK MEMBER

▪ GETTING OFF ON THE RIGHT PAW ▪

▪ LILY ▪

Photography: Kevin Neary

When bringing a new puppy home, be prepared to allow a full week of adjustment and transition to the new surroundings. Being uprooted from his environment and suddenly placed in an unfamiliar location with strangers, and strange new smells is indeed stressful for a young puppy.

Sometimes it's just as stressful for an older adoptee. Making the environment as friendly as possible will greatly help the transition.

Try to plan the homecoming just before the weekend, or when it's possible to take two or three days off from work. This will help the puppy adjust and feel more secure. Otherwise, at least postpone bringing him home until one complete uninterrupted day can be spent with him. He will absolutely need some guidance and reassurance. Interact calmly with the puppy, allowing him to explore the new environment with safety and reassurance. During the first week, or transition time, the following introductions are recommended:

1. a collar (buckle or snap—not training)
2. a short (4 ft.) leash—allowing it to drag behind the puppy. **No pulling or yanking,** and
3. house-training—typically involving the use of a crate. Quickly getting a dog used to the presence of a leash and collar helps reduce the occurrence of phobias and serious resistance to these tools. Furthermore, for practical reasons, there will be instances when you'll need to guide the puppy quickly away from certain areas or activities. Having a leash already attached makes for a practical "handle" on the situation.

Having to step around a leash may seem a bit of a nuisance, but consider the following case:

A 4-month old Pug with a particularly stubborn disposition, had yet to be introduced to any collar or leash, despite the owners having had him for nearly two months. After the initial consultation, the owners were encouraged to get him used to a collar as quickly as possible. They promptly went out the next day and purchased one, placing it immediately on the dog. Upon returning one week later for the first lesson, much to my surprise, the dog was *still* psychologically adjusting to the collar. The owners informed me that simply buckling the small leather collar into place had sent the dog into wild gyrations, frantically attempting to get it off. Finally, the dog settled himself behind a large armchair in a rather despondent and indignant state. There he remained for the next several days, having to be coaxed out for feedings and bathroom runs. While this is, admittedly, a very extreme reaction the point of the story is to put the collar and leash on the dog right away, so there will be plenty of time to adjust. By the way, there was a happy ending for this Pug, as he did finally relax and was able to learn all his commands.

▪ Constructively Enjoying Your Puppy ▪

Bonding with your new puppy or dog is of the utmost importance, and will start from day one. Bonding that is constructive and enjoyable for both dog and human, and yet not destructive to establishing leadership is very important. There is a way to achieve this with a dog that serves both purposes.

It's hard **not** to enjoy a new puppy — their cute little waddles, their bouncy demeanor and their delightful padding around behind you, watching your every move. And, of course, they're constantly inviting you to play with them. They'll chase your feet, chew on your hands and shoelaces, and jump all over you if you happen to sit within reach. This can be amusing for awhile, but eventually getting bitten, scratched and perpetually pestered can wear you down.

Read and learn by heart the finer points of passive messaging covered in Chapter 3, especially the sections on affection and game playing. This will undoubtedly help to explain the dynamic of what you'll likely be seeing over the next several days and weeks. If an owner is striving for leadership and obedience, the most constructive approach is to think of yourself as replacing the *authority* figure in the dog's life—not just the playmate.

There are ways to interact with a puppy without mixing signals or encouraging unwanted behavior. They may appear difficult at first, but the pay-off down the road is definitely worth it.

A) Remember that "petting" is nurturing and reinforcing behavior. Many people consider this to be one of the primary reasons for getting a dog—physical affection and closeness. Who *doesn't* just want to pet and cuddle with their dog? However, think critically about what the dog might be feeling when offering to pet or praise him. Touch will nurture and encourage the behavior and/or the state-of-mind the dog is experiencing at that moment. Unfortunately, too much physical stimulation can often overexcite a dog, quickly turning the encounter into a mouthing or biting situation. Again, the critical question to ask is "What was the dog's state of mind when the petting began—calm and relaxed, or playful and energetic?" And if the dog *was* relaxed at the onset of petting, was it possibly too prolonged, thus resulting in a case of over-stimulation?

B) Except during times when the puppy is calm, avoid sitting or rolling around on the floor with him. Avoid rough play and games like tug-of-war. As much as possible, stand or sit above him during interaction, especially if his mood at the time seems very energetic. From the dog's perspective, this makes the human appear as an authority. If there are young children in the house, explain this to them as well. Over the years, a few of my students have had to receive stitches in lips, ears and cheeks simply because they were too close when the puppy was in a very playful mood. If children insist on playing on the floor, try to get the dog or puppy focused on something else.

C) If the puppy does get too mouthy, (sometimes this happens even without any human encouragement) stop petting or interacting with the dog, telling him firmly "No!" Fold your arms firmly against your chest, keeping hands and arms away from the puppy's mouth and face. Refrain from petting for at least 5 minutes, or until he's calm. If he's particularly persistent, give a quick pop on the leash (remember the one he's supposed to be dragging around the house?) and say "**No!**" Sometimes it helps to pass an "okay" chew his way, but not always. You may even need to get up and firmly walk away from the dog for a period of time. Refuse eye contact as well during this time. By deliberately refusing to interact with him, an owner can demonstrate displeasure with his rambunctious outburst. Do not hold the dog's nose shut as this is very uncomfortable for the dog and often produces an even more "snappy" reaction when you finally let go.

D) "Fetch" is an all-time favorite with dogs and humans. When playing it, however, hold firm to the rules. This may mean that the game of "Fetch" could come to a screeching halt after only one throw if the dog doesn't bring the toy back and release it without a fight. **Don't** chase after the dog to get the toy. **Don't** get into a tug-of-war match to get it back. If the puppy returns with the stick but hasn't quite mastered giving it up, there are ways to teach him. Get hold of the toy with one hand, gently forcing the fingers of the other hand into his mouth to get him to relax his grip. Say "Drop" as he releases it. Or, try *gently* holding onto the back of the dog's neck/scruff (Chapters 3 and 4) with the free hand, while your other hand is holding the ball. Again, say "Drop". Do not release the scruff hand *until* the dog has let go of the ball. Give lots of praise for this. Trade-offs can work as well—i.e. give the puppy something *else* as a "trade" for the stick—a biscuit for instance.

E) Discourage the dog or puppy from leaping into your lap at will—this goes for whether you're on the floor or sitting on a sofa or chair. This behavior from the dog signifies a lack of respect for "personal space" (also covered in Chapter 3). High ranking dogs claim "personal space", and those who wish to enter it must do so respectfully. If not, they're likely to get disciplined in some fashion. Your lap or the furniture you're sitting on is your "space". You "own" it and others must wait for an invitation and/or be polite when entering. When dogs acknowledge higher rank in others, they are less likely to invade personal space in a disrespectful manner. Rebuff the dog if she jumps assertively (even in play) into your space. Teach her to sit and wait to be invited in. This is ultimately much more pleasant, especially if you own a large breed dog. Establish the boundaries early.

F) Do not allow the dog to sleep in bed with you. This, like the last item, addresses personal space. Leaders typically don't sleep in the same location as the subordinate members. It's more common to see dogs of *equal rank* sleeping together. Making the bed off-limits simulates one more canine behavior that might help in establishing a position of authority. For the sake of bonding, dogs can and should be invited to sleep in the same room with their owners whenever possible. However, a dog bed on the floor should be adequate. In most cases, this is close enough.*

G) Bond with the puppy through training exercises. This could be the single most important daily activity with your puppy. Unlike any other activity, training exercises are a team effort, working toward a common goal. Furthermore, the positive reinforcement she will be receiving will be "earned", and, hence, of much greater value in her eyes. The puppy learns what's expected of her, being given valuable praise and guidance along the way. It's what she craves—learning her place in the pack. And with just a few minutes a day, it's possible to see a change in a puppy's behavior and attitude.

• House Training •

This is probably the first big stress of a puppy's young life. Rest assured, all dogs survive this—and so do most owners.

There are two primary goals in housetraining. Teach the dog to: 1: hold her bladder until the right time *and* location, and 2: if #1 isn't possible, *let someone know!*

*Some people thoroughly enjoy "snuggle" time with their dogs before turning off the lights. This doesn't necessarily violate the personal space issue, as long as the dog was *invited* onto the bed. Also remember to adhere to *separate* sleeping spots when the lights do go out.

The following guidelines should help to make this as simple as possible for both you and your puppy. Be patient and above all, be consistent. Most puppies take at least a few weeks before they start to become solidly reliable. Don't be surprised if the puppy seems "house-trained" when at home, and then regresses during that weekend at the mountain cabin. Changes in schedule and/or floor plans (exit routes) can throw young dogs off course temporarily. These are usually minor set-backs and easily overcome.

A) Introduce the backyard or bathroom area first.

Most dogs will have to eliminate fairly soon upon arriving home. Stay outside with her for awhile, encouraging her to confidently explore the new surroundings. If you're fortunate enough to have the puppy actually go to the bathroom during this session, immediately attach a word or phrase to it, such as "Good go potty!" or "Good job!" with lots of praise. After that, the puppy is *probably* safe to go into the house for some *supervised* exploration. Show the puppy her water dish. No food need be offered yet. She will likely not be interested anyway.

B) Restrict pup to smaller areas <u>with supervision</u>.

A small area can be a gated-off kitchen or a portable exercise pen. Too much freedom in the beginning usually leads to more confusion and more accidents. Most people opt for confining the dog onto linoleum or hardwood surfaces as much as possible for the first few weeks until there is solid success in housetraining. For practical purposes, try to keep the "exploration area" close to the exit door to the backyard or the puppy's bathroom area. **Stay with the puppy** as much as possible in case he decides to try going to the bathroom again. Keeping him within sight is sometimes no small task. Invariably, when your attention wanders, that's when accidents happen. Always try to take the pup out through the same door so "the way out" becomes firmly ingrained in him.

C) **Keep the leash on the dog.**

Having the leash already on the dog in case of accidents will greatly increase the ease and speed of corrections, including getting him outside quickly to the proper area. Speak to the dog **firmly,** grab the leash and move **quickly**. Try to avoid yelling at the dog as this may result in him bolting away. If you're successful in actually interrupting the action, and getting him outside within a matter of moments, you'll have greater success. Once you're outside, **don't stop** until you're actually *in the designated bathroom area*. Now tell the dog to "Go potty". Chances are slim to none he'll finish his bathroom at this point, but don't get frustrated. Keep persisting with this same course of action with any future accidents. **Do not** leave the leash on the dog when he is alone or in the crate!

This approach can be used even if you live in a small apartment on the 17th floor and are forced to use potty pads. Make sure these are shown to the dog first, before allowing exploration.

D) Clean up accidents thoroughly.

Residual odors can send confusing messages to a puppy about where the bathroom spot is. There are good products available to remove the discoloration as well as the smell of pet urine and feces. You may even rinse afterward with a light solution of white vinegar and water. In extreme cases, for stubborn house-training dogs, have the carpets professionally cleaned and deodorized.

E) Pick up water dishes no later than 7:30 PM.

This will help ensure the puppy goes to bed with a relatively empty bladder. Since there will be no access to fluids after this time of the evening, don't engage in a lot of energetic evening play sessions that will leave the pup thirsty. Evenings are for calm, relaxed time before bed. Along this same vein, avoid free feeding of the puppy. Have set meal times, picking up any leftovers within a few minutes. This makes it easier to predict the *when* of bathroom runs.

F) Use a Crate.

In addition to rigid supervision and restricted areas, use of a portable kennel or airline crate is strongly encouraged. They can help in three main ways. First, it forces the dog to learn bladder control over several hours, as a normally healthy dog will not soil his bedding area. Second, if the bladder can't be held any longer, the dogs learns to indicate his need in some way, i.e. whining, barking, scratching, etc. Third, it all but eliminates puppy destructive behavior, preventing it from becoming a habit. When the pup is alone, he will be in his crate.

Remember, the crate should NEVER be associated with punishment. All too often, dogs are put in the crate *after* there has been an accident or when he's been caught destroying something. This is the wrong approach, and is likely to develop a negative association in the dog's mind with the crate. The goal is to have the dog view her crate as a safe and secure spot. Dogs are denning animals by nature, therefore sleeping in a confined space seems more natural to the dog than you might think.

One caution regarding crates: except for night -time sleeping, don't leave a dog in a crate for more than 3-4 hours at a time—*especially* in the beginning. If you must crate the dog during work hours, try to get home at lunch and let him out to stretch and walk. An 8-10 hour day in a crate is excessive and will make any animal a little crazy.

When selecting a crate, the idea is not necessarily to go with the biggest one simply so the dog won't feel cramped. If a crate is too spacious, the dog can effectively soil at one end and retreat successfully to the other, hence nothing is being gained. While crates can be costly, buying one with too much room can defeat the goal of bladder control. Wire cage crates can be modified down in size by slipping a barrier halfway back. Perhaps a mid-size crate is a better option, or maybe a friend can loan you one. The important thing is that there are ways around the size and cost factor of these items.

The introduction of a crate should be done in as

non-threatening a manner as possible. Avoid connecting it with punishment or a sense of isolation. Dogs will adjust more quickly to a crate if they still feel "part of the pack"—even while inside it. During the day, the crate should preferably be in a room where there's a lot of activity. Kitchens and family rooms are good options. The point is to teach the pup that the crate is *not* to ostracize him. Place an old towel or rug inside it for the puppy and possibly one of his chew toys. If the crate is inside another, slightly larger enclosure, you may leave the door open for him to explore at his leisure. When it's nap time and the pup is ready for a rest, use the crate. This time, however, *close the door.* **Offer no food or water in the crate!**

Unless the dog is older and already used to sleeping by himself, expect to relocate the crate (or, if possible, have a second one) to a bedroom at night and place it near the bed. **Under no circumstances should the dog be allowed to sleep in the bed with you.** Having the puppy near you at night will greatly speed up his overall adjustment to the crate. The first night sleeping without contact from siblings may produce some anxiety in the dog, but if it is handled calmly, he will relax. Bringing the dog into the bedroom allows him to smell and hear you. He knows he's not alone. If he wakes up whimpering during the night, soothing him can be done quickly and efficiently. In some cases, owners (including myself) have been known to sleep on the floor right beside the crate the first night. In this way, fingers gently inserted through the crate can provide reassurance to the dog. Try *not* to open the crate up and remove the puppy as part of the soothing. Chances are, it will be a struggle to get him back in!

Expect to take the puppy out once a night for the first several nights. After that, begin to encourage him to hold his bladder a little longer each time. At the first middle-of-the-night whimpering, tell the pup calmly but firmly, "No. Be quiet." Then try to get him to wait another 30 minutes to an hour. At the second warning, take the pup out. This same routine can help extend his wake-up time, so the pup learns to follow **your** schedule. Of course, this takes practice and time. Many puppies start to make it through the night within the first week. Some even get it after the first night. You may be one of the lucky ones.

In any case, **do not** turn the middle-of-the-night bathroom run into a play session. This trip outdoors is for **one reason only**. Once the pup has gone to the bathroom, it's back into the crate as quickly as possible. Offer no water or play toys. If he starts to yip or whimper for attention, tell him firmly NO and try to ignore him.

If, after several nights, the puppy is still a persistent whiner, you may opt for a stronger reprimand. Many students have had success with a little squirt (*not mist*) from a water bottle. In many cases, it can be a sufficient deterrent in the middle of the night. Give the pup a little squirt on the nose as you say "No! Be quiet." Place the bottle on the floor in front of the kennel, or set it on top in case a second reminder is needed. This usually works so well that after one or two days, simply showing the bottle to the dog, while saying "No!" gets him to quiet down.

If the puppy becomes immune to plain water, go to a 50/50 mixture of distilled white vinegar and water. This solution is completely safe and non-toxic. Vinegar diluted to 50% won't damage nasal passages or eyes. The idea is simply to produce something just unpleasant enough to get the dog's attention. Nothing more than that is generally needed, especially if you hold firm against the pup's attempts at manipulation.

G) Set a schedule and try to stick to it.

Dogs are creatures of habit much like humans. Establish a fairly predictable schedule with set wake-up, bathroom, feeding, exercise/ training and play times. For example, upon waking, first take the pup outside and encourage him to go potty. First runs of the day are usually successful, so offer abundant praise. He should preferably do **both** bathroom duties. Once that's accomplished, bring the pup inside, offering breakfast and fresh water. Remain in the same general area with the dog, in case he tries to wander. Feeding areas should be within easy access to the exit doors.

Some dogs need to be let out *in the middle of their meal*, so be watchful for this. Otherwise, take him out again as soon as he's finished. Play gently and constructively with him for a short while, perhaps 5-10 minutes. If he goes again, praise him. If not, bring him inside. At this point **do not** attempt to stimulate play any further. If obedience training has begun with the puppy, now might be a good time to fit in a practice session. Once this is finished, perhaps another 10 minutes or so, take the pup out one more time. If all is going well, finally allow the pup up to another 30 minutes of interaction and exploration. Total elapsed time for this may be 1 or 2 hours. At that point, the pup is probably ready for a nap or "down" time.

Don't allow the puppy to sleep anywhere he feels is cozy—it's too easy for him to wake up, wander off and get into trouble, without you being aware of it. If he has had enough time for all his "necessaries", then *use the crate for his naps during the day*. Place the pup in the kennel (in the *day-time* area) and *close the door* — no food or water. He may have a chew toy or toss a treat inside to encourage his entry. Allow him to fuss a little, but don't give in right away and let him out. If he didn't go to the bathroom within 30 minutes prior to being placed in the crate, you may opt to let him out *once* in case he's actually trying to communicate a need. Take him directly to the bathroom area and encourage him to do his business. Be prepared that the whining may have been nothing more than a manipulation attempt. If that's the case, place him back into the crate and this time be firmer. Do not succumb to manipulation. If it's a bluff, **don't fall for it!** At this point, consider the vinegar/water solution.

This same regimen can be repeated 2-4 more

times over the course of a day for each successive feeding/exercise/nap time. Obviously, the more successes you have outdoors with him, the stronger the routine and the pattern will become. Stand outside with the puppy when encouraging him to go. Leave nothing to chance or assumption! It's always best to have actually observed the activity.

H) Reward with verbal and physical praise, not treats.

Many is the time a dog has learned to "fake" going potty, just to get more treats. This includes asking to be let out every 15 to 30 minutes for the same reason. Be discriminating when judging the dog's requests to be let out.

I) Resist the urge to let the dog out every thirty minutes.

While a lot of books suggest this, and it may actually reduce overall "accidents", it isn't *teaching* the dog two very important things: 1. *holding* her bladder and/or 2. *letting the owner know!* when she has to go out. In a way, it makes it too easy and convenient for the dog. Owners that do this are more accurately training themselves rather than the dog. If the dog never has to communicate her needs, what has she learned? Mistakes aren't fun, but they are an essential part of the learning process. If you wish to let the dog out frequently, try to cut back to once every 2 hours during the day. This is a good start.

J) Leaving doors constantly open: not necessarily a

good idea.

This ties in with the previous suggestion. Furthermore, it can reek havoc with the heating bill if house-training is occurring in the dead of winter. Dog doors fall into the same category—too little control too early in the game. Leaving a door open for the pup may seem an easy solution *for you*, but it isn't teaching the dog to *let you know he needs to be let out*. Another problem is the assumption that, every time the dog goes out, it must be to relieve himself—highly unlikely, especially if he's constantly going in and out. Assuming anything at this stage is dangerous. Best to be standing out there with the dog, carefully observing to make *sure* he's gone to the bathroom. Once a dog is solidly house-trained, there should be no issue with either open doors or dog doors.

Many people leave doors open during the warm summer months, figuring they've got house-training licked. Then, when winter comes, they find accidents near the door, and sometimes all over the house. If that's the case, go back to the crate training, keeping the leash on and restricted access to certain rooms with rigid supervision. The dog's first attempts to let you know may be as subtle as sitting quietly beside the door. If you're attentive and praise/reward him for this, he may be more patient next time, perhaps even to the point of being vocal or coming to get you.

Don't overreact or jump too quickly to correct

or reprimand a pup who is just sniffing around. I had one student once who did just that and the house-training became a long, arduous ordeal with a very confused, frightened puppy. Rather, use the "sniffing" behavior to your advantage in the training. If you see that your dog is "looking for a place to go", encourage him a little, but then get him outside as fast as possible!

K) Never correct after the fact.

What do you do if you let down your guard and find an accident after the fact? The truth is, no matter how frustrated you might be finding another puddle, correcting a dog in any way *after the fact* serves more to release our stress over the mess on the floor than to teach the dog anything. Let's look at it from her perspective. If you drag the dog over in order to "point it out", she will immediately be tense and nervous because she's being pulled. While it's *likely* she may recognize her smell, it's very *unlikely* she'll remember producing the puddle or pile, especially if it happened several minutes ago or longer. And that is the very point. For a dog to fully grasp the concept of "acceptable/unacceptable behavior", corrections must be *absolutely connected with the action.*

The best reprimand you can give a dog in housetraining is to actually catch him **in the act.** Grabbing him at that very moment in time, dealing firmly and decisively, telling him **NO** and getting him outside as rapidly as possible has a far greater impact on teaching him the best spot to relieve himself. Again, always take the dog out through the same door, so he learns where he needs to go to get your attention.

Through all this, one must remain calm and understand that the puppy is not doing this intentionally. After all, his Mother didn't seem to mind where he went, and she quietly cleaned up after him. This will doubtless be your puppy's first biggest stress in his new home. Some pups seem to pick up on this faster than others. I've known some dogs to start to "get" this in less than a week, while others are still fighting it after a few months. A lot has to do with persistence and awareness of the dog's whereabouts. This can't be stressed enough. Don't give the new pup more room and freedom than he can handle until he has learned the rules of housetraining.

Before moving on, the major points to remember in housetraining are:

A) Introduce the bathroom spot first.
B) Allow exploration only in small areas under strict supervision. Too much freedom too quickly results in more accidents.
C) Keep a leash on the dog.
D) Clean up accidents thoroughly.
E) No water after 7:30 PM.
F) Use a crate—and not just for night-time sleeping.
G) Set a reasonable schedule and try to stick with it. Dogs are creatures of habit, too, so use that to your advantage.
H) Reward verbally.

I) Resist the urge to let the dog out constantly — leave room for "error" in the teaching.

J) Don't leave doors open for *your* convenience. You will likely be creating another problem that may require re-training down the road.

K) Never correct *after the fact.*

▪ Socialization and Fear Stages ▪

There are a couple of issues that should be touched on when specifically dealing with puppies: they are the fear stages (there are two) and working around them to successfully socialize your dog.

There is irony in the fact that the puppy's most pronounced fear stage, between 8-10 weeks of age, coincides almost exactly with his prime *socialization period*. How does one deal with that? Can you let your puppy play with children, other dogs, etc., without traumatizing or emotionally scarring him? The answer is an obvious Yes, but how to do so may seem puzzling.

When selecting a potential playmate for a puppy, try to choose one that's of comparable temperament and sociability. Puppy's that are within 2 weeks of age are better potential partners. Size doesn't *necessarily* effect the decision unless it's a huge difference. The reason age rules over size is because we are looking for puppies who are at the same level *developmentally*. One puppy at a time as a playmate is also easier to handle, less overwhelming and intimidating. Know the puppy and, for health reasons, be sure both have had at least two sets of puppy booster shots. Select a clean and non-threatening environment for them to play and investigate. Don't overdo it, either. If it appears that one puppy is getting tired and frustrated, call for a time out. Sometimes just a few minutes of play can go a long way.

Follow the same guidelines when introducing children. Infants and toddlers are not the best as they can't be guided very well by **you** on how to properly interact with the puppy. Also remember *one child at a time* when it comes to petting the puppy. Visualize what it looks like to a young puppy with an entire group of kids all coming at him at once! If a child frightens or over-stimulates a puppy, they could get bitten out of fear or through aggressive play.

Avoid exposing a very young pup to extremely loud noises. This can have a very negative effect on him, imprinting an anxiety that might last for months or longer. Fireworks on the 4th of July are consistently a problem for young dogs. You may opt to leave town for the day with your pup if it coincides with that 8-10 week fear stage. In a pinch, a basement or quiet room in the house may work, too, to keep the noise level down. I don't recommend sedating the dog as a precaution unless you are fully cognizant of a pre-existing fear behavior linked to loud noises. If the goal is to help the dog overcome his problems, then he needs to be *fully aware* of his surroundings, not in a "drug-induced" state of pseudo calmness.

The second fear stage hits at around 4 months and also lasts a couple weeks. It's usually not as pronounced as the first one (the dog's susceptibility to trauma) but by no means should you ignore it.

In any case, common sense is the best rule of thumb. You can't NOT socialize your dog because of the fear stage. Over the long haul, you're missing the best opportunity to introduce the pup to the world at large. Be smart about it. Take the pup for walks in quieter areas, but do take him for walks. Introduce him to children, just not the 25-year family reunion. In general, use common sense and a bit of planning.

CHAPTER 3

WOOF DID YOU SAY?

▪ DE-MYSTIFYING DOG LANGUAGE ▪

▪ SHERMAN & MURRAY ▪

Photograph: Author's collection

For the purposes of this book, dog communication will be separated into two categories, referred to as "passive" or "active". "Active messaging" refers to direct communication, usually the teaching of a command. It is teaching a dog to associate a word (command) with an action. "Passive messaging" involves more subtle communication that goes on throughout the day. Passive communication is so important and so powerful to building the right relationship with your dog that it will be the major focus of this entire chapter.

This one area alone is where most people fail when it comes to communicating effectively with their dogs. It's also where many training programs fall short, because they lead people to believe that the key to controlling the dog is solely in teaching commands. This can easily become a false sense of security. No doubt commands are essential in constructively channeling the dog's mental energy, but the true key to leadership is in passive messaging and being consistent in your behavior when interacting with the dog during a normal day. It really has little to do with words or "command". In a natural setting within a group of dogs, positions of authority and rank are established without the use of "speech" as we define it.

In the simplest of terms, unless an owner demonstrates pack authority over a dog, the animal will typically feel no "obligation" to respond to commands—certainly with no degree of reliability or consistency. One doesn't become that authority figure by simply teaching hundreds of words to the dog, or necessarily "getting tough" with the dog. That position is primarily achieved through proper *passive messaging* and projecting the right energy and body language to control the situation—no matter

what that might be. When dealing with your dog, are you calm? nervous? fearful? tense? relaxed? aggressive? stressed? frustrated? passive? confident? ambivalent? confused? A dog can sense any one of these emotions, and will react accordingly.

• Passive Communication's Power •

Dogs, as do many animals, have an ability to pick up on another creature's emotional state. Whether that's your "aura", your "vibe", or your "essence" you don't need to tell the dog how you feel—he can sense it. Dog owners are often amazed how an outsider or third party, (i.e. the trainer) can produce quick results with their dog, when they can't seem to get him to do anything. This can demonstrate the power of passive messaging. A good trainer should know how to put a dog at ease, not mix signals and get him to acknowledge their higher rank, at least for the duration of a training lesson once a week. This same ability to sense emotions can be observed between dogs. If one dog senses fear or insecurity in another, the more dominant animal may choose to take advantage of the situation, viewing the other dog as a potential easy target. Using this understanding of energy is critical in establishing a functional rapport with your dog. An attitude of calm confidence makes all the difference in the world if you want your dog to accept you as the leader.

Just as easily, human behavior/actions can nurture a state of mind in the dog that *hinders* learning. Ask yourself when your dog seems *most* responsive to direction—when he's full of repressed energy?

When he's tense or nervous? When he's playful and rambunctious? Or when he's calm and relaxed? If you answered the latter, you're correct. If, through proper passive messaging, you can put him into that frame of mind, how much more productive and rewarding the time spent with the dog will be. Try to operate on the idea of a "two-way mirror", being conscious of how your actions appear to the dog. He doesn't miss anything. Project a calm, relaxed, but confident demeanor. Make him feel the same and he will put all his trust in you as the right authority for him.

During a particular consultation with a couple, I was greeted at the door by a husband and wife who realized their 6-month old Great Dane mix was out-of-control. The other "greeter" was the culprit in question. During the first 20-30 minutes of the consultation, the dog displayed his usual antics—for which I had been called in. He lunged forward and back, aggressively inviting me to play; he challenged me with confident and prolonged direct stares; he even occasionally tagged and barked at me in more defiant demonstrations of his prowess. Through it all, I maintained a cool, disengaged demeanor, not looking at the dog or responding directly to any of his displays, even turning my back on him at times. While it took nearly a half-hour, he finally realized I wasn't to be moved. He then became quite passive, attempting to get my attention with a completely opposite approach in his behavior. He calmly laid down beside me, gently laying his head on my knee. It was at that point that I turned and acknowledged the dog with calm praise.

This is a very dramatic example of how the right energy and body language can actually have a ripple effect, rubbing off on the dog. It also shows how a dog will pick up relatively quickly on a calm, dignified presence that demonstrates leadership qualities. Some folks might view this "cold shoulder" behavior as mean, but I assure you, the dog's feelings weren't hurt. He and I simply communicated on a different level than he typically got from most other people who came into the house. The most important thing to note, though, was that I never said a word to the dog!

Remember that any kind of *positive* interaction with your dog is taken as a reinforcement, potentially encouraging and nurturing the behavior observed at the particular moment in time. We have all experienced the unbridled exuberance of a puppy when someone comes to the door. She is excited, agitated and full of expectant curiosity and hope. The door opens and the first thing that happens is the person on the other side notices the puppy. "Oh! Whaaat an adorable little fur ball! She's soooo cute!" etc., etc. Within seconds, all control of the situation is lost, human and dog are mixed into one whirring mass. This enthusiastic response (from the human) is seen by the dog as a definite reinforcement. Does this combination encourage calm, attentive behavior? Through the simple act of petting or even making direct eye contact, the human nurtures this dramatic display at the door.

You might say, "It's only a puppy." Or perhaps you might make allowances if it's a breed that will top out at 10 pounds. But...puppies *grow*. Furthermore, you wouldn't likely be making excuses like that if it were a 150-pound Rottweiler or Akita at the door. A dog is a dog, and out-of-control behavior is simply that, regardless of how you wish to excuse or explain it away. Think about how your actions appear to the dog. Don't respond or reward the dog if the behavior you're seeing is ultimately unacceptable. Guide him into a calmer, more relaxed state of mind — then reward that!

What defines "positive reinforcement" will vary from dog to dog, and situation to situation. Dogs with extremely rambunctious personalities can often feel they are being encouraged to play when an owner (thinking they are rebuffing and "correcting" the dog) repeatedly pushes them back. Too often this simply appears as a delightfully physical roughhouse session, exactly what some dogs live for. Knowing your dog's personality is absolutely critical to deciding the proper response to a situation.

▪ Communicating *Beyond* Fear ▪

This rule regarding positive reinforcement holds true as well, even when a dog reacts out of fear. When a dog is nervous, anxious or insecure, resist the inclination to protect, comfort, or soothe. We often do this without even being aware of it. The dog is nervous in a social setting, quivering with anxiety and tension. We bend down and start to pet the dog, telling him "It's okay." What, exactly is the *it* of this message that is *okay*? Not what you might think! In these situations, all the dog is aware of is his anxiety and fear. Dogs do not *express* their emotions so much

as they *live* them. Therefore, what *he* understands is that his feelings, his state-of-mind, his fear at that moment, is the ***it***, and apparently you approve of it. His emotional state is being validated and supported simply because the owner is responding directly to it, possibly even petting the dog (nurturing behavior). It can get worse with small dogs, as many people simply scoop them up when aggressive or fear behavior is observed. By "protecting" the dog, he is prevented from learning how to deal with a situation on his own. Small dogs are no less capable than other dogs in handling stress. By not "rescuing" him all the time an owner can encourage their dog to become self-confident and relaxed, trusting them and their leadership.

When a dog is feeling nervous or insecure, a more productive, helpful approach for the social/psychological growth of the dog, is simply to channel his attention into something that can calm him and take his mind off the fear-object. This can often be done by working hard on the "Stay" command. Regular exercises with a variety of challenging situations combined with obedience can help the dog redirect his attention and relax a great deal.

▪ Killing with Kindness? ▪

The affection factor is, without a doubt, the biggest culprit of all when it comes to passive messaging. It seems we are constantly loving on our dogs. Sometimes it's demonstrated with pure physical emotion, other times by vicarious purchases that are supposed to translate as love and "appreciation". The dogs absorb it all, also using this behavior as a means of determining their rank. When it comes to physical affection towards your dog, ask yourself some hard questions: Do I pet him because he's "earned" it with good behavior, or am I just petting him because he's the greatest dog in the world, no matter what? When he's pestering for attention, will any amount satisfy the dog, or is it similar to the behavior of an addict, always needing more? When he's stressed, does he run to me for validation or protection, and do I immediately give him a reassuring pet? Do I continue to try and pet him, even during out-of-control behavior, including biting?

If you can identify with any of these situations, then you likely are overly affectionate in dealing with your dog. Don't misunderstand me. I'm **not** against petting or loving your dog. Rather, the point is that constant fawning over a dog is often the "back door" to climbing the social ladder. It doesn't produce calm obedience—in many cases, excessive affection creates a spoiled brat attitude. Remember, a dog draws his sense of pack position from *your* behavior. Within the wolf pack, the only dog that gets such constant fawning attention is the leader. Explained in another way, think of affection as just another "resource", or "commodity" controlled and divided up equally and fairly by the leader, something that, ideally, should be *earned.*

Few people understand the insidious effect of excessive petting on a dog. In a slow but undeniable way, it can, over time, elevate the dog's status. It can

also create unnecessary jealousy between pack members, where one feels she isn't getting her "fair share". The following actual cases involving excessive affection and an overly protective attitude serve to clearly demonstrate how one can defuse aggressive and/or uncooperative behavior, re-directing a dog's motivation in more constructive pathways. It can be done in many cases by taking a deliberately and purposefully "passive" stance, or by being "emotionally selective". By cutting out the "fuel" (petting and/or affection) for the behavior, it can often go away, deprived of the oxygen it needs.

A few years ago, an elderly woman with a 4-month old toy poodle contacted me for training. The dog had an undeniably strong-willed and confident personality. Unfortunately, it was hopelessly cute and everyone around had a hard time resisting her. The dog quickly took charge of anyone and everyone, receiving near constant affection and praise, regardless of whether she was sweet and docile, or feisty and aggressive. The attitude of this dog was evident in her lack of reliability with the obedience training. To begin a calming process, I advised the owner and all those with whom the dog was in regular contact to cease petting her for a few days. After one week of modifying the "affection factor" this little dog became dramatically more docile and respectful to all around her. Affection became a much desired resource, as opposed to an "entitlement". Petting could then be gradually resumed, but only if the dog was demonstrating appropriate behavior, i.e. *earning* the affection.

A couple with a 1½ year-old Shih Tzu complained of seemingly aloof, distant behavior from their young dog. They felt he "didn't need" them or their attention. Almost cat-like in his behavior towards them, he came around sporadically, asking to play, but when they tried to initiate the interaction, he seemed almost standoffish. The attitude was also apparent when it came to the "Come" command, as no amount of coaxing seemed to get this dog to respond. They were afraid they had the most non-interactive dog on the planet. It became apparent that this little dog never needed to "ask" for attention. The owners were overly indulgent on this score, thus the dog became super-saturated from the affection. They were encouraged to withhold physical attention for one week and take note of any change in behavior. They were allowed to greet the dog briefly and then just ignore him except for training sessions. Within just 4 days, the dog was completely different in how he responded to the owners. Allowing the "tank to run dry" forced this Shih Tzu to realize how much he did indeed need interaction with other pack members. The young woman even commented that the dog began following her around the house, lying at her feet between activities—something he had never done before.

Lastly is the case of a 10-month old Chihuahua who was displaying increasingly aggressive behavior, having actually bitten two people. The behavior was typically directed at, but not limited to, children. One of the two people bitten was, in fact, the owner. At the initial consultation, the dog displayed extremely insecure behavior, avoiding me and constantly jumping at the owner's legs. She

typically responded by picking the dog up and holding him in her lap. He would be content for a few
moments, then want to get down. Over the course of
an hour, this behavior cycle repeated itself over and
over. At no point did the dog show normal social curiosity and attempt to approach me, in spite of the
fact that I did nothing more threatening than to sit
across the room and quietly talk with the owner. After the second training session (and after I had become bite-victim #3) the dog's behavior remained
largely unchanged, except that he showed more apprehension and timidity in my presence. At that
point I directed the owners to abruptly cease petting
the dog, picking him up and/or carrying him
around. In short, completely control the "affection
resource". This was a tall order, as the 8-year old
daughter adored the dog. Nevertheless, they duti-
fully followed the suggestion for 11 days, during
which time the only positive interaction the dog received was brief verbal praise associated with appropriate behavior and commands. Otherwise the dog
was largely ignored. By the end of the 11 days, the
point had been made and the dog had essentially
stopped the aggressive behavior. To my knowledge,
the biting has not returned. This dog had successfully learned to use the owners' affection to build his
sense of "pack rank" and shelter himself from the
outside world. Whenever he felt threatened, the
owners were there to protect and defend him from
all the "scaries" out there. However, when his protec-
tors failed in their duties, he found the ability within
himself to reach out, learning to interact with non-
pack members. Furthermore, he no longer received

affection regardless of his conduct. Affection was now something he had to "earn" for appropriate behavior.

After observing how easily and dramatically their dogs' behavior could be altered by *not* doing certain things, all of these people were able to resume physical affection and praise—but with a new awareness and respect of its powerful affect over the dog.

• Game Playing •

Another major culprit in passive messaging is game playing. Many people, it seems, purchase dogs so they can relive childhood playtime by engaging in physical activities with their pet. I've watched people roughhouse, play fight, tug-of-war, wrestle and chase around after their dogs. Regardless of which one of you begins the activity, the passive message is still the same—confusing roles. Let's look at these activities as well from the dog's point of view.

Within a group of dogs, these games are frequent—especially with puppies. They are one way dogs learn social skills and how to interact effectively with each other. However, there is an underlying message that can't be avoided if one is going to play along. The dog sees that all participants in the game are essentially *equal to one another in the social hierarchy.* These types of activities are largely observed in the "beta" group of the pack—those dogs that aspire to being the leader. As they "practice" on one another, one of the purposes is to determine a victor. Whoever wins, at least for the moment, has the upper

hand, possibly gaining another foot-hold in his climb to the top. Doesn't sound so bad on the surface. Some people still play these games, making sure they always win. But the underlying message is still confusing to the dog, and the behavior doesn't mimic the leader's when you watch a pack interact.

There are many "wrong" messages your dog will pick up if you play these games.

1. Within a pack, leaders know better than to compete with subordinates. His dominant position is not up for grabs, and he conducts himself accordingly—calm and dignified. Rough and tumble games are for the youngsters, the followers and the status seekers in the pack. Further, a mother dog (alpha to her puppies) with a litter must, for the sake of survival, have the pups' complete respect. Again, this is a situation where the boss doesn't confuse roles by giving mixed signals.

2. Rough play tells the dog that rambunctious, possibly contentious behavior is acceptable. He will undoubtedly make social blunders and initiate this type of behavior with others outside the pack. Let's hope it isn't the elderly next-door neighbor, or the wobbly toddler down the street.

3. By allowing a dog to win such games, he, at least for the moment, assumes a superior position over you. It may be a short-lived game, but with repeated "wins", the dog's higher rank becomes strengthened. The cumulative effect is that, over time, a dog can easily turn into a tyrant, often becoming aggressive when he doesn't get what he wants.

I always advise my students to be cautious when instigating a romp session with their dog. Depending on a dog's individual personality and the stage of the training, these types of mixed signals might have no impact on the overall performance. Then again, it may profoundly affect the relationship. Once a dog has firmly accepted their owner as the leader, the rules governing these activities become more relaxed, but will always be viewed as a mixed signal to a greater or lesser degree.

In summary, be aware of *how* you interact with your dog. If you're not sure how your behavior is being perceived, observe the dog. Is she calm and relaxed, or is she running around, jumping, barking and biting at everything? It's possible you may have produced this condition by the messages you've sent her. Remember, your dog will largely be a product of how she perceives you, which behaviors get reinforced and which do not.

Beyond affection and game playing, there are many other ways that body language helps owners and dogs understand each other. There's an old saying that "a picture is worth a thousand words". With that in mind, imagine your dog's body (and yours as well for that matter—from the dog's viewpoint) as the picture. Learning what different gestures and postures mean, owners become more attuned to their dog's perspective, energy and focus. It also helps immensely in knowing when *your* efforts are connecting with the dog, as well as when his attention and motivation are directed elsewhere.

The scope of this book is too limited to cover all the minute intricacies of dog gesturing. For a more thorough handling of this subject, try *Canine Body Language, A Photographic Guide,* by Brenda Aloff, *The Dog's Mind,* or *If Your Dog Could Talk,* both by Bruce Fogle, and/or *Dog Language, An Encyclopedia of Canine Behavior,* by Roger Abrantes. For the sake of brevity, this book will focus primarily on those gestures and behaviors that demonstrate authority and/or passivity. It is critical to know when a dog has acknowledged an assertion of higher rank. She will *signal* you with a demonstration of what is called a "pacifying" or a "yielding" gesture. An owner who doesn't recognize these gestures might inadvertently overemphasize a point with the dog. The long-term effects of ignoring these gestures can be an excessively timid or fearful dog, one who doesn't trust others or her own ability to effectively communicate. Therefore, learn to "read your dog".

• "Reading" the Dog •

The following are some of the most basic and easily observable gestures that dogs use to communicate their emotions and intentions. An owner should be alert to them at all times.

Posturing Assertive dogs display their positions of authority by *shifting weight and balance.* A confident stance is fully erect, often appearing stiff and rigid. The balance of the dog's weight will be shifted forward onto the shoulder area. The head will be held high, indicating confidence and alertness.

Weight shifted towards the rear with a backward-leaning posture indicates submission or in extreme cases, fear. When holding a leash, stand tall with shoulders back and your head up. Try to make your movements smooth and fluid, not choppy, indecisive or ambiguous. To a dog, such a posture speaks confidence and calmness, rarely intimidating, but rather instilling trust in your leadership qualities.

Leaning/Standing Over the other Dog This gesture is considerably more assertive than simply standing tall and erect. The more assertive animal attempts to place his head and/or shoulders leaning over the other dog. It is a more direct display of dominance, rarely seen as a polite gesture. If this behavior is observed during an initial greeting, or shortly thereafter, it may produce a confrontation if one dog doesn't back down quickly. Small dogs can also attempt this gesture, possibly requiring them to balance on their back feet, especially if the other dog is much larger. Be alert to attempts by your dog to stand over you or a younger member of the household, i.e. a child. This sometimes happens when people sit on the floor. Your lowered height in such a situation can invite a status-seeking dog to try this behavior.

In general day-to-day interaction, deliberately leaning over a dog to make a point usually isn't necessary. It may happen occasionally during a correction, that an owner finds himself leaning over the dog. There's nothing incorrect with that, in fact it may, depending on the situation, psychologically add to the effectiveness of the correction. At other

times, though, if the dog appears nervous when you stand or lean over her, approach this gesture cautiously and with discretion.

Mounting This behavior is both dominant and sexual in nature. Males will of course attempt mounting females who are in heat, but at other times the behavior can be observed between dogs of the same gender, or females mounting males. Hence, it becomes apparent there is another meaning to the display. This behavior might be tolerated between two dogs who know one another fairly well, but, like the *leaning-over* display, mounting is generally regarded by dogs as pushy and impolite. It might also provoke an aggressive outburst from the recipient. Towards humans, this behavior should never be tolerated. Never allow your dog to mount you, a family member or any other person. Spaying or neutering a dog often eliminates mounting as higher hormonal levels can tend to precipitate this behavior.

Pawing at the air or one another can mean a number of things, depending on the context. A larger dog who abruptly places a leg/paw over the other is attempting dominance. Seen as a rather assertive move, it can lead to play or a possible challenge/face-off. A paw held slightly off the ground or even to chest height is often a friendly greeting and can precede an invitation to play. A paw held slightly off the ground for several seconds conveys submission or anxiety. If this is the case, there will be other "signals" as well. (This should not be confused with the "point" display with hunting dogs). The paw may remain held slightly in the air, or cautiously be extended towards you. The dog may attempt to touch you tentatively with the edge of the paw.

Ears Ears can be moved vertically or laterally and signify many different things between dogs. It matters little the design or shape, all dogs have the ability to rotate or shift their ears along the side of the head. Also be aware that ears can and do change positions in a split second, indicating a sudden shift

pups in dominance play   Image courtesy Bennett & Hastings

in the dog's motivation and state-of-mind. Be alert to these sudden shifts and practice "reading" the dog's ears. Dominant and/or alert ear position is up and fully forward on the dog's head. When holding the leash and working with the dog, look to see whether the dog's ears are alert and forward. If so, then follow the dog's gaze. Hopefully, he will be looking at *you.* If not, then he's likely fixated on something else. If this fixation lasts more than a few seconds, encourage the dog to redirect his attention onto you. (This requires some guidance with training technique and skill.) Fear or extreme anxiety is often indicated by ears that are positioned as far back as possible and flattened against the skull. The goal of training should never be to produce these extreme emotions in the dog. Respect from the dog is appropriate—fear is not. The ideal ear position when training is half-way

ears indicate confident, alert and curious state of mind.

Image courtesy Bennett & Hastings

ears in more submissive but relaxed position.

Image courtesy Bennett & Hastings

back and gently folded— indicating a calm, submissive yet attentive state-of-mind. The dog is aware of her surroundings but primarily focused on the owner and what is being asked of her.

Eyes Dogs' eyes are very expressive and are often a good way to judge personality and temperament. Dogs' eyes can express fear, calmness, trust, excitement, submission or a fierce challenge. Like humans, a dilated pupil indicates adrenaline in the system, meaning intense emotion, most likely fear. Visible ridges around the eyelids also indicate stress and anxiety. Narrowing or blinking eyes are yielding gestures. Fully open and relaxed eyes indicate the same with the dog's mind.

Eye contact when training should be encouraged. Many situations can be enhanced by getting the dog to look directly at you. Beyond the training "gaze", there are primarily two things to be aware of with eye communication. First is the direct stare, often taken as a challenge. It can be playful or aggressive, *depending on what the rest of the body says.* If you sense a definite aggressive stance from a strange dog, do not attempt to "stare him down". In all likelihood, this will only make the situation worse.

The next situation is when a dog deliberately and purposefully *averts* his gaze. Refusing eye contact is primarily done for one of two reasons. First, it can be a pacifying gesture initiated by the subordinate animal. This can often be observed when a higher ranking individual (possibly an owner) is disciplining or asserting rank over another dog. The lower-ranking dog acknowledges the gesture, and signifies as much by breaking eye contact. Be alert to this gesture, as it's usually a good indicator of "when you've connected with the dog". I've had many students who, upon seeing the dog look away, became frustrated, thinking the dog was ignoring them—this is the "human translation" of the behavior. One fellow told me he repeatedly pulled the dog's head back around each time it looked away, sure that his dog was rudely snubbing him.

The other situation when eye contact is deliberately withheld is completely the reverse — the higher ranking dog refuses to look at the lower ranking individual. The rest of the body language also displays assertiveness and confidence, but the final link in the communication process (a direct gaze) is denied as a way to keep the upper "paw".

Tail Tails, more than any other body part, are the quickest way to determine a dog's motivation and state-of-mind. It's possible to "read" a tail from a distance, even if the rest of the dog's body is unclear. Unfortunately, some breeds have no tails (i.e. Australian Shepherds and Cattle dogs, for instance) and others have tails with reduced maneuverability (i.e. Pugs, and those with very closely cropped tails). If your dog fits these categories, fear not — learn to pay more attention to the other signals, just as a blind person relies more on smell and hearing.

In this discussion of tails, it is important to be aware of the "normal range" for a particular breed's tail configuration. For instance, Huskies normally carry their tails lifted high over their backs with a full curl. Relaxed or assertive, the tail generally stays as such. Beagles and Fox Terriers carry their tails stiff and erect, like a flag pole. This does not mean they are constantly attempting to assert themselves. This is their "normal range" in most contexts. My German Shepherd Dogs have easy-to-read tails, generally relaxed and carried low, unless they become aroused. Know your breed's bench-mark for configuration!

Nevertheless, one of the most important parts of tail communication is the *elevation*. Tails held low indicate calmer, more submissive states-of-mind. Tails held high are a confidence barometer—the stiffer and more elevated—the more alert and assertive the message. Tails held tightly between the legs and against the belly indicate timidity and fear. *Wagging* of tails is a secondary message to the above. Tails can wag in any of the aforementioned positions. A wagging tail **does not** necessarily indicate friendliness. Instead, it's more an indication of the *intensity* of the dog's emotion. The arc of the wag is critical. Short or long, if you can tell that the tail is making a wide arc with the movement, it is usually a relaxed, friendly signal. Tails that wag with a stiff, narrow arc are indicative of a more cautious and/or assertive state-of-mind. Thus, a dog approaching with a rigidly erect and stiffly wagging tail could very likely be issuing a warning, not a friendly gesture.

Then there is also a gesture commonly called the *Body Wag*. This is impossible to miss. It's the old "tail wagging the dog" situation. If anything indicates enthusiasm and friendliness, this gesture does the trick. The dog approaches the other person or dog, moving his entire body in a back and forth, "wagging" gesture. The head will also typically be held low during this.

Personal Space This refers to your actual body and the immediate surrounding area—chair, sofa, or even floor space. *How* a dog enters the personal space of another can indicate social status. Subordinate dogs approach leaders with deference, gesturing with submissive body language. Touching is done in a respectful manner—usually involving sniffing, brushing past with the sides of their bodies and some licking. Playful approaches are considerably more rambunctious, indicating the youth and generally lower status of the participants. When two dominant animals enter each others personal space, the body language is alert, stiff and on guard. Rarely will they take their eyes off one another. It's also typically a head-on approach, keeping the "weapons" at the ready.

A dog who invades the personal space of their owner in either of the latter two scenarios, (and repeatedly gets away with it) most likely does not view the owner as higher ranking. Owners who allow or even encourage their dogs to jump onto them are not asserting respectful behavior when it comes to personal space. In fact, a dog that demands attention by jumping and repeatedly pawing at people without being corrected can easily learn to manipulate and eventually dominate those around him.

Personal space can be reduced or extended, depending on the circumstances. High ranking and/or assertive dogs will often extend personal space, aggressively warning off others from getting too close. This is often seen, but not limited to, defense of territory.

Which dogs assert personal space and for what reason is important to note. A leader is privileged to enter any pack member's space at any time and for almost any reason. A *follower*, however, isn't given the luxury of setting up boundaries against the *leader*. Dogs will assert personal space against those of *equal or lesser rank*. Never tolerate it if your dog tries to keep you at bay! To do so sends a bad message and can only develop into something larger and potentially more dangerous. I've heard far too many stories of how owners abruptly backed down when a dog growled at them simply because they moved too closely or touched the dog when it was napping. If you observe behavior like this, seek professional assistance, and/or seriously examine **all** the passive messages the dog has been receiving for some time.

Remember that even though owners are meant to hold higher ranking status over the dog, this does not mean we should display disrespectful behavior when moving into the dog's space. Leaders observe and are sensitive to rules of etiquette as much as others. This doesn't negate what was just mentioned about "standoffs", but, by the same token, humans shouldn't abruptly and unceremoniously pounce on a dog, especially if he's asleep or intent on something else. To do so can all too easily evoke a natural "startle" response, often culminating in someone getting bitten.

The <u>invitation to play</u> is an almost universally recognized posture. One dog will "bounce" down on her front paws, hind end up in the air. Fearful, overly aggressive or very assertive dogs almost

never display this gesture. If your dog is willing enough to invite another into play, it shows a friendly social curiosity that is generally appealing.

Rolling onto the Side is the ultimate display of submissive gesturing. Rolling onto the side will also be discussed in Chapter 4 in the topic of corrections, but at this point it's important to include it because this behavior is often seen when dogs interact. With this gesture, a dog will submit voluntarily to an older or more dominant animal. Dogs who have been over-corrected or abused will often do this over even a slightly raised voice. The behavior shows the subordinate dog dropping and rolling onto his *side* in front of the other animal. The dog on the ground may remain there for several seconds, or until the other animal begins to back off. The subordinate animal may also produce a small amount of urine in the process.

The dominant (standing) animal thus sees the other as no threat, hence maintaining his superior rank. Pups will typically offer this display for any and all elders. Having limited or immature social skills, it's simply easier to "play it safe".

This behavioral gesture shouldn't be confused with a personality assessment technique in which pups or dogs are rolled onto their *backs* and held down. The two positions are neither synonymous nor interchangeable. Except under very limited conditions, training should not require the dog to display this level of submission. There are many gestures we, as humans, can acknowledge and accept as sufficient indicators of the dog's subordinate rank.

Hackles The hair raised along the spine is often seen in dog interaction. Elevated hackles will make one animal appear larger, perhaps intimidating the opponent. Raised hackles do not automatically mean there will be a fight, but caution is always a good idea. It is caused by an involuntary reaction in the dog related to the presence of adrenaline. It often occurs with, but is not limited to, encounters between unfamiliar and/or assertive dogs. Except with a stranger or an interloper into the pack area, a truly confident high ranking dog rarely needs to add this "extra" to his already assertive body language. Therefore, it can also be seen to some degree as an indication of the dog's insecurity with the situation. The more relaxed the dog is, the less likely it is that the hackles will rise. An interesting note to this gesture, though, is that I've watched the hackles go up with my own dogs when they are simply engaged in play. Since there are never any serious conflicts between my dogs, and, furthermore, they certainly "know" each other quite well, I suspect, in this situation, the hackles simply add a degree of excitement or intensity to the interaction.

Whining Originating from puppy behavior — signaling distress or anxiety — this is something that dogs commonly do as a way of communicating stress, fear, or frustration. It is also something that owners often complain about with their dogs. First of all, it must be understood that whining is *not crying*. Dogs

do not cry. To respond to it in that fashion, as a parent to a child, is probably one of the main reasons dogs become conditioned to whine. Previously in this chapter, it was stated that any kind of positive interaction with the dog will be taken as reinforcement, potentially nurturing and encouraging the behavior or *state of mind* of the dog at that moment. An owner who is constantly trying to soothe a whining dog will eventually have a dog that never stops whining. While completely ignoring the whining isn't recommended, either, use some common sense about it. Doing exercises that channel the dog's mind in other ways is often the most constructive approach to curing the persistent "whiner".

Voice Dogs do use their voices in communication. We should, too. There is a distinct difference in tone and pitch between a friendly yip, a bark of boredom or frustration, and the low, threatening growl. When speaking to the dog, pitch is important. In many situations, lower tones tend to get a dog's attention quicker. Modulate your voice accordingly to help add emphasis to the situation. If the goal is to keep the dog calm and focused, the voice should be even and tempered. On the other hand, if the voice is being used to encourage and reinforce, make it as enthusiastic and sincere as possible.

Try to avoid having a "conversation" with the dog. Notice that commands are one word—typically one syllable at that. Keep it short and sweet. On the whole, the dog will respond more to *how* something is said, as well as body language cues, than *what* is being said.

▪ Putting It All Together ▪

It is critical to remember that a dog will signal his feelings and intentions with more than just one body part. In other words, a dog will never say he's fearful with *just* a tucked tail — there will also be indications from his ears, eyes and shifting of weight towards the rear. This knowledge of dog "signals" and how they affect behavior is absolutely essential if one wishes to be a more efficient handler and trainer.

How one responds to any given situation or "signal" should be based on the emotional state of the dog and his degree of understanding of the command in question. The time one has to respond to these signals will vary. Sometimes it will be a few seconds, sometimes only a split second. In either case, it is much easier to respond with an attempt to re-direct the dog *before* she has *acted* on her emotions. So be alert! Some time ago, taking a walk with my oldest female, we encountered another person walking a very energetic, adolescent Boxer mix. This dog was determined to "say hello", and the owner didn't or couldn't prevent the greeting. My dog, Lily, didn't really appreciate the abrupt and enthusiastic invasion of her "space" by this other dog. She stood patiently for a few seconds, as I watched the muscles of her face draw back, the ears shift and her eyes grow narrower. The Boxer, either oblivious or too young to care, did not withdraw. As I started to re-direct my dog, I also strongly urged the other owner to get her dog back, but she couldn't react fast enough to avoid the quick warning snap from Lily.

WOOF DID YOU SAY? ·

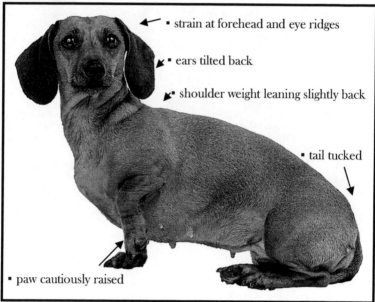

· strain at forehead and eye ridges

· ears tilted back

· shoulder weight leaning slightly back

· tail tucked

· paw cautiously raised

Image courtesy Bennett & Hastings

PUTTING IT ALL TOGETHER

above: Daschund signaling "submission" in a variety of ways
below: Golden Retriever pup signaling confident and assertive
    frame of mind.

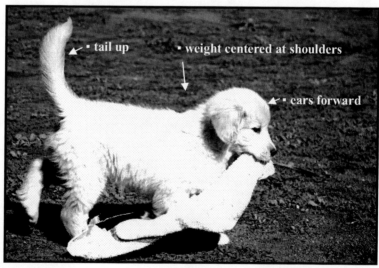

· tail up   · weight centered at shoulders

· ears forward

©Istockphoto.com/paule858

As you go through the rest of this book, then, learning more about training, techniques, how they should be applied, and specific exercises, it is important to always be observant to the dog's language and what she is speaking to you. Do not always assume you know what the dog is intending unless you have thoroughly "read" her *and* the other dog, if there is one. A wonderful place to practice your dog language skills is a dog park. Going *without* your own dog may be beneficial as it is easier to be just an unattached observer. Take notes and see if you can identify the gestures outlined in the preceding pages. You will be amazed at how quickly the dog's world will open up to you.

CHAPTER 4

ACTIVE MESSAGING

▪ DIRECT COMMUNICATION AND THE TOOLS TO HELP YOU ▪

▪ HOMER ▪

Photography: Randy Morrison, Electra-Eyed Productions

Active messaging is the other half of the communication process between dog and owner. In Chapter 3, it was stated that dogs achieve leader status without the use of speech. For us, then, as humans, active messaging translates in practice with how we handle our dogs during training. Active messaging means communicating directly to the dog—channeling his mental energy as well as how to respond if the dog disobeys or becomes seriously distracted in spite of your efforts. It is establishing word association in the dog's mind with specific behaviors and actions (commands or rules). The "how-to" of teaching commands will be dealt with in later chapters. In this chapter, active messaging will be covered that involves guiding, encouraging, demonstrating, praising and, last but not least, *disciplining*.

▪ In Praise of Praise ▪

Which form of positive reinforcer one chooses is subjective and will vary from dog to dog and situation to situation. Hands-down, the preferred item is food. There is no argument that 99% of dogs out there might just try to fly to the moon for the smallest crumb of food. But that's not the point—or maybe it is... Obviously if they're willing to do that, one has to ask "why"? It stems from the dog's view of food as opposed to the human's. To humans, food is associated with social activities, food is art, food is *love*. So, the more we dish it out, the more we love our dogs, right? Dogs, however, view food as simply a basic need for survival, a resource, and nothing more. This need can be manipulated in the training process, but it can all too easily get out of hand, leading to contentious or aggressive behavior.

There are potentially some very real "backlash" behaviors that can result from relying excessively on food as the primary motivator. First, as mentioned earlier, it keeps the dogs too "hyped-up" for the sake

of *obedience*. I deal frequently with dogs who have developed food aggression, selective responsiveness (based on presence or absence of the treat) hyperactivity taken to an extreme, or just plain boredom (this last issue often requiring the owner to come up with a "bigger", "better", "shinier", "yummier", etc., etc. motivator) all stemming from too many treats in the training process. The decision *not* to rely on treats, at least for me, then, is based on knowing that *they simply aren't necessary* to get good results, and that there are other very effective alternative motivators available. It isn't about wanting "power" over the dog. It's about lifting the dog's mind, and my relationship with him, to a higher level.

Toys as a motivator are somewhat less common, but still can be effective. I've used them more for bored dogs than anything else. If the dog seems to get more "pumped up" for training if it's fun, then one can sometimes "act" it out, rather than use the toy. Nevertheless, effective training should always be open to modification and flexibility for the sake of the dog.

Clickers are a popular device for positive reinforcement. Initially, they are used in conjunction with either food or a toy, so the dog will associate the sound made by the clicker with something positive and/or rewarding. The clicking sound, in training jargon, is referred to as an **"event marker"**. Dog hears the sound at a precise moment, connects *behavior or action* with sound, as well as reward immediately following the sound. Thus, the clicker also becomes a positive "directing" device that keeps the dog's attention. Though they are gaining in popularity, and there are many books that will guide the owner on the "how-to" of clickers, I do not use them.

Dogs are social by nature and are sentient beings. They experience and exhibit emotions themselves, and respond to emotions in others. To a degree it is a trait known as "**allelomimetic** behavior" (monkey see, monkey do) but there is more to it than that, as not *every* dog will respond exactly the same, and not in *every* situation. An entire pack can be calm and relaxed, napping on a sunny afternoon. Suddenly the alpha alerts to a potential threat. He stands up, stiff, alert and ready. The rest of the dogs notice immediately and in the blink of an eye, they, too, are on alert. The same thing can be observed at a dog park with young dogs playing and romping. The energy is quite infectious and will have a ripple effect on those around. This ability in dogs to notice and respond to each others emotional states can and should be used in training. But it must be genuine.

The power of praise in the training process shouldn't be underestimated. It also should not be looked at as just a momentary response for a single action. It is more an overall manifestation of a positive attitude towards the dog. Praise should flow in a natural, enthusiastic way as you handle the dog. A dog can spot a phony a mile away, so don't be one. When training and throughout the day, offer affection, praise and encouragement when the dog is showing his best. The most effective demonstrations

of praise come from the heart, and are exhibited by the whole body—face, arms, and voice. At times, praise can have a definite playful feel to it, encouraging the dog to respond in an animated, energetic fashion. In lieu of *using* biscuits, I've been known to tell my students to "*be* the biscuit".

Some trainers claim that simply praising a dog as the reward for a job well done is insufficient and ineffective. However, more than two decades of living this philosophy with my own dogs and those of my students proves to me the opposite. Using emotion and praise to motivate and inspire a dog seems to hit its mark more than a food reward. Yes, there is the occasional stoic, unresponsive, aloof dog that takes all my enthusiasm and just stares back. On those occasions, flexibility is the rule of thumb, including psychological approaches that may help the dog get in touch with his need for social contact.

Always try to keep an even balance between praise and encouragement (positive reinforcement) and the occasional correction (negative reinforcement). This helps keep the whole process as fair as possible, ensuring the development of mutual trust and respect between both parties—dog and human. There is a profound difference between learning how to *lead* a dog as opposed to simply dominating her. The former acknowledges that both participants can learn from one another in an atmosphere of openness and genuine appreciation. It addresses all the needs of the dog.

▪ In Defense of Discipline ▪

If the definition of "correction" is anything that does not *encourage* a behavior, then it opens a wide range of possibilities. Back in Chapter 1, it was stated that dogs generally don't continue repeating behaviors if they see no obvious benefit to it, or if it is met with a sudden negative consequence. Further, in Chapter 3, the discussion of "passive communication" was discussed, asserting that this, more than "active communication" (corrections) is primarily how dogs establish rank. While few dogs will reach the top without some amount of sparring, the idea that the way to the top is through "corrections" only is unjust and also highly inaccurate. With this in mind, I've found in practice that body language, maneuvering, "protocol" exercises that serve as a way to control a desired "resource", eye contact, voice, and sometimes psychological approaches are quite effective in many cases, thus limiting the necessity for more traditional or direct corrections. Hence, a view of discipline that allows only for *physical* deterrents is too narrow. The owner should feel free to draw on a full repertoire of responses, depending on the situation.

The use of discipline in dog training carries much controversy. This one issue alone seems to put some trainers in earnest blood-sport against each other. Methods that oppose the use of corrections often use descriptive and emotionally based terms that evoke a visceral response. While the argument and the words chosen may be debatably just a battle of semantics, one is either okay with the idea of corrections, or not.

Nevertheless, a brief discussion of terms might be appropriate. The very word "punish" pre-supposes an emotion attached to it, possibly conjuring up visions of abusive techniques. Furthermore, "punishment" implies an attempt to impose guilt or remorse for an action—something dogs are completely incapable of experiencing. "Punishments" can also occur long after an alleged transgression, effectively destroying the issue of *understanding consequences*. I've also come across the words "aggressive", "hostile" or "angry" in the discussion of discipline. If one really understands dog behavior, it becomes easy to see why these terms are inappropriately applied in the context of a reasonable training program. "Aggression" can imply an *unprovoked attack* and hence has no relevance to a properly executed and *controlled* correction when applied in an obedience setting. "Hostility" and "anger" are emotionally based and lead to visions of lack of control in technique and execution. Again, it goes back to discipline *starting* with the owner.

On the other hand, to "correct" infers no emotion whatsoever. In plain terms, one does not punish or get hostile towards a child for misspelling a word — one simply "corrects" and moves on to the next one. The corrector keeps the correction relevant to the incident, and there is no stigma attached to it. "Corrections" are a daily occurrence in pack life.

Realistic and fair discipline should be seen as a natural response on your part to guiding the dog back on track to acceptable behavior—and there is a difference between a "correction" and simply "distracting" a dog's attention. From a dog's perspective, corrections are part of how his psyche is programmed — trial and *error* again. Oddly, most owners have little problem watching their dogs interact with their canine kin. This often involves some pretty physical encounters, as dogs learn to stand up for themselves. Why is it, then, that when it comes to *us* standing up for ourselves in front of the dog, we get weak-kneed and ambivalent?

As a human being, we may like the notion of being able to completely avoid confrontation with another creature. To a dog, however, the idea of "discussion" in some situations is inappropriate and foreign. A mother dog doesn't "ask" the pups what they think about wandering out of the safety of the den. Discipline is meted out as a necessity for the survival of the pack. If all members behaved like a loose, squabbling rabble, the pack would collapse from the inside out. On the other hand, proper discipline ensures that the pack will function as a well-oiled machine, continuing to survive. When done with fairness, control and judgment, disciplining the dog, in his eyes, can be seen as a show of strength and foresight on your part, looking out for his welfare as well as the pack in general. He'd get at least that much from a fellow canine.

Lastly, "discipline" and/or "corrections" (specifically the ones following) come with a word of warning. Before considering the following types of direct actions, *please* make sure you have thoroughly read, understood

and are implementing proper *passive messages* to your dog. It's very hard to justify correcting a dog for so-called "bad" behavior if he's simply responding to the rambunctious or confusing messages from the owner. In other words, if *we're* not disciplined with our behavior, how can we expect it from the dog? If one continues to act the role of playmate or "fawning servant," then the dog, in all fairness, might not legitimately be considered *disobedient*, but simply *confused*. The purpose of language and effective communication between two individuals is to reach an acceptable level of understanding and compromise, thus *avoiding* conflict whenever possible. Energy wasted in conflict is to neither the owner's nor the dog's advantage. Proper communication on all levels usually solves or, at least, greatly reduces this.

One of the concerns people often have about discipline is the fear that they'll hurt or psychologically scar the dog. This boils down to technique and training, reading the dog and using good judgment in deciding a course of action. That's where a good teacher or training book is a big help. Just doing "any old thing", as long as the dog stops the behavior, is not reasonable. Supporting the theory of corrections doesn't mean *any* old correction. There are very few that I personally will consider as fair and reasonable.

The purpose of a correction is not to hurt, inflict pain, or produce fear in the dog. It should only be to get and re-direct his attention quickly, and in the process, help him to understand some degree of negative consequence for a particular action. The best corrections are those that *get through to his psyche* on a primal level, the goal being to develop *respect*, not fear. This is the main reason why striking the dog does more harm than good. Not only does it inflict unnecessary pain, it *makes no sense to the dog.* He cannot relate to it other than as a fear producing stimulus. Dogs do not hit, strike or lash out at one another repeatedly and for no apparent reason. They do not scream and yell at one another. Such methods in training or in life serve no purpose and can only undermine the trust you want the dog to have in your authority. In such situations, the "end" certainly does not justify the "means".

Another concern people have about discipline is the notion that the dog "won't like them anymore" if they're firm with him. This is simply a myth. When a dog accepts leadership as legitimate and fair, and, further, understands the rules and that he has violated them, then an occasional, controlled correction does not create fear or foment rebellion against you. In fact, as time goes by, dogs who view their owners as fair and benevolent leaders will bond on a much deeper level than with "playmates". My dogs are delighted to see me (and I them) when I get home every day—they hover and greet and demonstrate affection for several minutes in a show of excitement and appreciation. They know that attention and affection received from one of higher status is generally considered to be of greater value than from a peer. Structure, rules and predictability are things that dogs instinctively seek within the pack. Give them this and they will be all the more content and fulfilled.

All this aside, people are, by and large, unsure about "how" to correct a dog. "Better to do nothing at all than risk 'ruining' the dog," is often what happens. Going from one extreme to the other, however, is no solution either.

A lot of the effectiveness and fairness with a correction comes down to four things:

1. Is the "energy" correct and tempered while you're doing it? In other words, does the dog feel you're confident (without going overboard) in your technique, or are you unsure, awkward and having feelings of self-loathing? Emotions can't be hidden from the dog. If you don't feel your leadership is legitimate, why should he?

2. Has it been presented in a *timely* manner so he can relate it directly to the behavior in question?

3. Is it *reasonable* to the mistake in question — minor error, minor correction?

    (Items 2 and 3 are especially important here, as they are often mentioned in relation to a phenomenon called "Predictor of Punishment", wherein a dog will become more reactive and agonistic toward a situation or distraction because she links it with an unpleasant memory of a correction that was badly timed or used excessive force. *Timing* and *judgment* are absolutely essential here.)

4. Is the correction something the dog can psychologically relate to? Does what you have done actually make any sense to him?

This last question is important in how it relates to dog behavior. The most effective corrections are ones the dog understands in his "dog realm". A mother dog doesn't wag a finger at a puppy. She doesn't scream, yell or lecture him. She doesn't give him "time outs". She doesn't spray him with Binaca. She doesn't smack him on the butt, or use a rolled up newspaper. She doesn't spend her day handing out kibbles to keep the pups in line. And if it's a potentially dangerous situation, she certainly does not turn her back on the pup and *walk away,* hoping he will notice and follow her before he gets into trouble. What she does do is growl, nudge, bump, snap, shake and possibly pin a pup onto his side. These are legitimate "doggy" corrections that your pup will understand. They are the most effective ones if you want to get through to your dog. They are never done to excess or with animosity. Mom's goal is not to hurt or injure the pups — after all, they're her babies. But, just as importantly, she understands their safety depends on how well they listen to her. Therefore, she doesn't hold back if a puppy is out of line.

Another critical issue relating to discipline is that once the correction is over, one must emotionally *move on.* All too often, owners will make the mistake of dwelling on a correction. Dogs don't carry grudges against one another. Missteps and corrections happen, the pack remains intact, and five minutes later everyone is getting along again. An owner must have the same attitude. While there will and should be *some* observable reaction from

the dog after a correction, it is counterproductive to see it as anything other than what it is—a natural response (typically submissive) to what *you* have just done. After all, if one individual is being the leader in the interaction, the only other role to play is the follower. The dog will "play his role" and signal his response with submissive body language. Allow this and don't overreact or try to "make-up" right away. The dog will come around quickly if you don't make a big deal about it.

Let's face it, discipline isn't the "fun" part of training. Everyone wants to spend more time on the positive reinforcement issues. But learning how to handle corrections properly will lighten the burden of having to do them at all. It also forces us to see the balance more clearly between the two sides (positive and negative) as the ultimate goal.

Selecting the most effective tools to guide and discipline the dog fairly and humanely is of the utmost importance. The next section will outline what's on the market currently, comparing and critiquing them. This will hopefully help in selecting the most effective equipment to do the job. The following sections on Tools and Corrections should be seen as information that will be used primarily in a "training" setting—that is, teaching commands or general good behavior. There are plenty of other situations, throughout the day, where dog behavior can be controlled by effective *passive messaging*, alleviating the need for anything more physical.

• TRAINING COLLARS •

There are a number of different collars to choose from. When making a selection, it should be based on the following criteria:

1. <u>What is the dog's temperament?</u> This is probably the most important consideration. Dogs, like people, are very individualistic. Their personalities and temperaments differ. If you've got an easygoing, mellow dog, you might be successful with a gentler collar, or even start with nothing more than a standard buckle or "snap" collar.

2. <u>What is your dog's size?</u> It's fairly safe to say that the bigger the dog the stronger the collar should be, if for no other reason than sheer strength and bulk. This is an important criterion, but I must add that just because the dog *is* large doesn't mean he's "tough". I've met more than my share of 100-pound. pushovers.

3. <u>Is the collar safe and humane?</u> To a large extent, safety stems from proper *use* of a tool. More accidents happen from misuse and abuse than anything else. This concern has a lot to do with the skill level of the person holding the leash, which leads to the next question—

4. <u>How adept are *your* handling skills?</u> If you're a novice, you might want to try a collar that works easily and effectively, allowing some room for error. Some collars can be "finicky" and require a lot more finesse and technique than others.

5. <u>Is the collar actually able to *teach* the dog through</u> the action and sensation it creates? This is a very

important item to consider. There is a big difference in the dog's mind between a device that simply "restrains", and one that actually "teaches" her to stop certain behaviors.

Finally, remember that these are "training" collars. In other words, once a satisfactory level of control has been reached consider downgrading on the collar, or even trying a regular buckle collar. If the dog doesn't start to regress in responsiveness, you've probably achieved your goal. Too many people get stuck in a rut, relying on "training" collars for prolonged periods when it's simply not necessary.

• Gentle Leader or Halti •

These are a head and nose apparatus that fit over the dog's snout. (This device is obviously ruled out if your dog is brachycephalic [blunt nose] as are Pugs, English Bulldogs, Pekinese, etc.) The leash connector is directly below the chin. The device tightens down around the nose when there's tension on the leash. Rated according to the above criteria:

1. It appears to be relatively effective with dogs who are mild to moderate in their temperaments. If your dog is a bit more vivacious or is extremely sensitive around his nose, this may not be a good choice — or it will require some serious getting used to.

2. There are different sizes in this item, but so far I've not seen any on very small dogs — under 15 pounds.

3. It is a safe tool on the dog. So far, there have been no reported injuries.

4. Fairly easy to manipulate if your skill level is average.

5. The general consensus is that these are used as a "restraining" device, not something you can use as a "correction". It's application is limited — mainly useful when practicing the "Heel". If the dog needs to be corrected for an improper "Sit" or "Down", you should use a second collar choice.

There is some benefit with this training device in re-directing a dog's gaze. It can be an efficient tool to break a dog's direct stare at an intended "target", as the eyes must follow where the nose is pulled. When handling a dog with known confrontational behavior, a gentle leader might be more effective than a collar, simply because the latter won't necessarily force the dog to break eye contact.

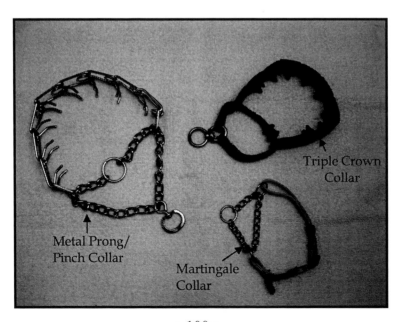

Triple Crown Collar

Metal Prong/ Pinch Collar

Martingale Collar

• Choke Chains •

1. On a *continuous* basis (that means not having to "upgrade" at any point during the training) I've had reasonably good responses with chokers on dogs with mild to moderate temperaments. If you've got a spunky little personality on your hands, an adolescent, or a very large dog with a huge, hairy coat, then you may be hard-pressed to get through to her with this.

2. Chokers come in all sizes, fitting dogs from 5 pounds to 205 pounds.

3. Because of their mild appearance, the assumption with these devices is that they are very safe on the dog. *Caveat Emptor!* Used improperly, these collars can easily scar, damage and/or collapse windpipes. Research and autopsies indicate these collars can do serious damage to dogs. I suspect it's largely due to lack of training or proper technique. So get some good guidance if you're a novice.

4. Chokers are a bit tricky to use properly. There is a definite right way and a wrong way to situate a choke chain on the dog. Hence, again, the risk of damaging the dog. If you're unsure, get some instruction! These collars do have a lethal aspect to them, so use them prudently!

5. Used *correctly* these collars can and do "teach" a dog right from wrong. However, if you feel your dog is oblivious to the corrections, I would encourage you to seek some good professional guidance and/or select a different collar.

Personally, choke chains are my *least* favorite training collar. I will avoid these more than any other because of their dangerous design and potential for injury to the dog's neck.

▪ Martingale Collar ▪

This is essentially a variation of a choke chain. It's typically made of nylon, having a section at the back that acts as the retractor, responding to a tug from a leash. The sensation is more a "tightening" than a "strangle". The rating on effectiveness is the same as for a metal choke chain, with the exception of Item 3. Unlike a standard metal choke chain, a Martingale collar has a "stop" design that prevents it from going ever tighter. Because of this, they are much safer and more humane, completely preventing inadvertent strangling of the dog. Metal choke chains have no actual stop point to the action—they can theoretically tighten to the circumference of a twig.

▪ Prong or Pinch Collars ▪

These devilish looking devices are designed with interlocking links, each having two slightly flared, angled prongs aiming inward toward the dog's neck. When pulled on, the links tighten as though hinged, superficially pinching the outer layer of the dog's skin or pelt. Pressure is *distributed evenly* around the neck. The sensation simulates a gigantic mouth, and/or the biting action of another dog. The tips of the prongs should be thoroughly rounded, smooth and blunt, thus eliminating the potential for scratching or other skin damage.

These, like the Martingale collars, have a special design which stops the tightening action of the collar, thus removing any possibility of seriously choking or damaging the dog. The idea behind these collars was to create a sensation (a bite) that would be comprehensible to the dog but not risk injury, as a choke chain does. In spite of the fact they've been readily available for at least a couple generations, these collars are still controversial. I suspect it's due to the *appearance,* as it conjures up images of cruelty and torture. Unfortunately, emotion seems to rule over logic with these collars, in spite of the fact that, as will be explained below, they are the single most modifiable training collar available. So here's how they rate with this trainer:

1. They have a high level of versatility, being able to be used on dogs of wide temperaments. There's a general idea that they're only for really stubborn or headstrong dogs. They can, however, be used on a wide variety of dogs, even small ones. I know they are kinder and gentler than a choke chain to the dog's windpipe and esophagus. A light correction can often go a long way. Nevertheless, unless a professional trainer has advised it, this collar should probably not be selected as your *first* choice. It is more commonly chosen as an "upgrade" if another collar is having no effect on the dog's responsiveness.

2. Metal prong collars currently come in four sizes, each of which is highly adjustable for a custom fit. They are adjustable for dogs from as small as 10 pounds on up.

3. For novice handlers they are much less finicky than a choke chain. I find them quite user-friendly. The only downside would be that with the larger sizes you'll need some strong hands/fingers to separate the links and slip them back together. (A quick-release design may be more appropriate.)

4. As stated earlier, these collars are quite safe when *fitted and used properly.* If you aren't sure how to use it, check with a professional or even the manufacturer. To get the best results you'll need to adjust it to custom fit your dog's neck. Studies that compared these collars to choke chains determined that when used and fitted properly these collars produced no injuries.

5. These qualify as an excellent teaching tool. The collar is to remain comfortably on the dog's neck until a mistake is made. It is then quickly jerked or snapped (*a little goes a long way!*) to get the dog's attention.

Prong collars, as mentioned above in Item #2, are to be "fitted" on the dog. **Do Not** attempt to slip the collar over the dog's head, risking damage to the eyes and/or ears. The proper way to place it on the dog is to "open" the collar by separating two like links (or buy the kind with a quick release mechanism). Then place it around the dog's neck, slipping the links back together. Links can be added or removed for custom fit.

The safety feature of a metal prong collar is a round ring referred to as the "dead" ring. It's located at the back, in the center of the retraction section. This ring stops the action of the collar, preventing it from going ever tighter, as a choke chain would.

properly positioned Prong Collar

Photography: Robert Neary

There are three tests you should use to ensure proper fit:

1. **The Finger Test:** A properly fitted prong collar should *comfortably* allow <u>no more than</u> 3-4 adult fingers to be slipped between the collar prongs and the dog's neck.

2. **The Slide Test:** A properly fitted prong collar should, with a *small* amount of effort, slide completely around the dog's neck. Using both hands, placed at opposite sides of the dog's neck, you should be able to slide it back and forth with minimal effort.

3. **The Triangle Test:** Once the prong collar is on the dog, pull gently back on the retraction portion until it comes to a natural stop. You should see a distinct triangle.

The pronged links should not be touching the "dead" ring. In fact, there should be a space of approximately ¾" or more between the dead ring and the first pronged link. This ensures the dog's neck, not the safety device itself, is stopping the collar's action. Once properly fitted, it is quite safe for your dog, and gives no discomfort just wearing it. A prong collar should *never* hang loosely or droop around your dog's neck. Check the collar periodically (every few days to once a week if you have a growing pup) and add links as needed to ensure correct fit. Packets with extra links may be purchased.

The adjustability features of these collars goes beyond adding or removing links. Any individual link can be *inverted* if you desire, limiting the "pinching" sensation to only specific points along the dog's neck. It's also possible to soften the *degree* of pinch, by switching the leash from the main ring to the "dead" ring, or both simultaneously, which will completely stop any tightening action.

When purchasing a metal prong collar, check the tips of the prongs. The manufacturer should have gently rounded the tips to a smooth, buffed edge. If you feel any burs, hang it up and test another one off the rack. The collar shouldn't *scratch* the dog, just *pinch* him. I've found the best quality prong collars are those made by the Sprenger Company, from Germany. If

your local pet supplier doesn't have them or can't get them in, they can be purchased on-line.

link inversion option on Prong Collar

As already mentioned, I do not typically recommend these for a first choice collar. Creating pain is *not* one of the criteria for a correction. There is no doubt there is pain felt with a pinch collar correction. *However,* it is relatively small and easily controlled with good technique. After all, a dog's thick, hairy coat is going to soften the pinching sensation greatly. (It won't feel the same if you try it out on yourself!) I have upgraded to pinch collars if a milder design isn't working. These collars are effective when used properly and if the need is there. They seem to work best with dogs who are within a normal range of emotional responses. That is to say, *not* a good choice for dogs who are highly reactive—excessively fearful or aggressive.

▪ Triple Crown Collars ▪

While I like the action of the prong collar, and the unique design does a good job simulating a "bite", some dogs just don't need the intensity of the metal prongs. Smaller dogs with big attitudes can benefit from this relative newcomer on the market. The action and design is identical to the metal prongs with the exception of reduced intensity and fewer adjustability factors. (You can't invert links or soften the pulling sensation.) Fitting these is identical to their metal counterpart. Triple Crown collars are *plastic*, lightweight and efficient. They can be even safer than a metal prong collar because the links are solid, so there's virtually nothing for them to snag on. I've had excellent results with dogs 45-pounds and under. I rate them side by side with the metal prong collars with a couple of minor differences:

1. Because the links are plastic, they aren't as sturdy. There's a greater likelihood of the hinges giving out on you. For this reason, I've been hesitant to use them on dogs of 50-pounds or more. If you think your larger dog could benefit from the prong design, go with the metal.

2. If your little dog has a thick coat (i.e. Pomeranian or American Eskimo) they may not actually feel the correction through their fur.

3. They are sometimes difficult to find. Not all pet retailers carry them. Ask around. (The brand name is key when searching.) They can also be purchased on-line.

The last four collars covered (choke chains, Martingales, metal-prong, or plastic-prong collars) are designed with a retraction section that can tighten on the dog. Specifically for this reason, they should *never* be left on a dog without supervision. The outcome can be tragic. Further, I make it a point to *remove them during play*. It's far too easy for metal collars to become entangled (a most unpleasant situation!) or for dogs to chew off a nylon collar. Use good judgment and *be attentive*!

• Remote Collars •

These types of collars are gaining in popularity and can be quite effective when the handler is trained properly on usage. They have been used successfully for many years for field training of hunting dogs. A small word of caution regarding these collars: dogs can easily become "collar savvy" with these (similar to prong collars) meaning their attentiveness is phenomenal when they know the collar is on and quite the reverse when it is removed. Watch out for behavior that demonstrates this attitude. If you are interested in trying a remote control collar, look for a reputable trainer in the area that can guide you for maximum potential and safe usage.

• LEASHES •

Leashes come in various lengths and styles. Any dog handler should be equipped with at least two leashes, preferably different lengths. For beginning obedience expect to use a standard walking leash, measuring between 4 and 6 feet. It doesn't matter what it's made out of, as long as it's sturdy and feels comfortable in your hand. It's a good idea to have an extra one on hand of about the same length for the dog to drag around the house — remember that suggestion in Chapter 2? This leash will probably get dirty and chewed, so don't buy an expensive one for this. (Chain leashes can be a good choice for this.)

For intermediate and advanced obedience, have a 20-foot leash handy. These can be purchased at most pet stores, or you can make them with a little ingenuity — 7 yards of nylon braid or webbing, a leash clasp from the hardware store and you're in business.

Retractable leashes for training are alright for some beginning obedience exercises, but be prepared with the other types of leashes for intermediate and advanced work. Retractable leashes seem to encourage sloppy or non-existent heeling. The Heeling Exercise itself is supposed to demonstrate your role as leader, as well as give the dog solid mental guidance and structure. If the intent is to "Heel" with the dog, you've essentially wasted your money with the retractable leash. It will just have to be locked in place, thus serving the same purpose as a regular 4-6' leash. Also be aware of the mixed message sent to the dog when she is allowed to wander back and forth, and side to side on a retractable leash. The dog may be getting some *physical* exercise, but very little *mental* exercise is occurring. Much more is achieved if the owner guides and directs the dog, challenging her to "follow your lead". And, once the discipline is achieved, it won't detract anything from the dog's overall enjoyment of the walk.

▪ MUZZLES ▪

While I always carry a muzzle in my "tool" bag, I rarely use them unless there is an absolute need. Furthermore, they are limited to use with dogs that actually have snouts (as opposed to blunt-nose breeds). A dog that's not used to a muzzle may become more fearful and aggressive as a reaction to wearing it. In light of that, be sure the tool is absolutely necessary for *your safety* before using it. Also, if the decision is made to use a muzzle during training, get the dog used to wearing it *when he's **not** being trained*. This follows the same line of thinking as having him drag a leash around the house. If a dog has a limited view of a particular tool, he will never relax about it and will likely be suspicious when it comes out.

There are two types of muzzles to choose from:

1. **Sleeve Muzzles** These are made of fabric (usually nylon) that slips snugly over the dog's snout, thereby eliminating his ability not only to bite but also to drink. For this reason, it should not be left on the dog for long periods of time or in very hot weather.

2. **Cage Muzzles** These are highly variable in design and material. They can be made of plastic, leather or wire. They should completely cover the dog's nose and muzzle area. There should be padding at the bridge of the nose to reduce rubbing and chafing. Air flow is also important to allow the dog to open his mouth for panting or drinking. Look for open designs. If you feel you need to buy a muzzle, do some research and try to actually *see or handle* a couple different styles before making the final decision.

Leashes and collars are a must for training, so select the ones that are most comfortable for you and most effective for your pet's temperament. Only a *very* small percentage of dogs will ever need a muzzle, especially if you start training at a young age and do it right.

• CORRECTIONS •

The following section outlines those corrections that are limited to leash corrections and direct hands-on techniques. Besides the more subtle ways that one can control a dog through body language, energy and passive messaging, these are the only techniques I use in actual training situations. They are used when the situation warrants it, after it has become apparent that other methods are not getting the desired response. *Always* use good judgment when choosing to use one of the following techniques. A correction needs to be immediate and produce a rapid (however temporary it may be) response. In a training scenario, for instance, a leash correction would be more appropriate for poor Heeling—as opposed to the psychological approach of ignoring the behavior. Safety of the dog is key here. Also be aware that if you are dealing with intense emotions from the dog (i.e. extreme fear, frustration, or anger) some physical corrections might be inappropriate, potentially escalating a situation. The following corrections are meant to be used in situations where the dog is experiencing a *normal* range of emotions.

A "correction" must have the following components to be reasonable and fair:

1. It must be timed to near perfection for best results, linking it to the unwanted behavior

2. It should be decisive but brief, lasting only a moment, sufficient to stop the behavior in question, *but nothing more.*

3. It should **not** be aimed at inflicting pain or suffering on the dog.

4. It should be a technique or maneuver that *the dog can actually relate to.* This implies that whatever one chooses to do to discipline the dog should, at the very least, mimic to some degree a behavior that we observe between dogs themselves.

▪Voice ▪

Another important point to stress is that corrections should not be done silently. While speech is the least important part of dog communication, it is critical to make *some noise* when you correct. It could be a grunt, a squeak, a bark, or, ideally, a word. But there must to be *something* the dog hears simultaneously with the correction. Thus, over time, a dog will mentally connect the noise made with the immediate negative consequence. Eventually, the sound alone will get the dog's attention, in most cases stopping the behavior. If, on the other hand, corrections are done silently there will be a distinct disadvantage when the leashes and collars come off. How, then, is an owner supposed to signal unacceptable behavior to the dog if she's half a football field away?

Corrections will be separated into three categories. Those in Category (Level) One are generally considered less severe than those in the next two levels. All levels of corrections will convey the concept of a negative consequence for an action. The decision regarding which "level" to use is based on the situation, the degree of the offense, and the skill level of the handler. A correction is supposed to redirect and control *the dog's mind* and what he is focusing on. *If one has control over the dog's mind, then the body will follow.* Keep in mind that one should always use the *least* amount of force necessary to achieve the desired response from the dog. As with most things in life, it's always best to start at the bottom and work your way up. The dog will appreciate it as well.

▪ Level One Correction: "The Collar Check" ▪

In addition to being consistent with all the "passive" messages, this is the best spot to begin when guiding a dog into appropriate behavior. In the beginning, for the sake of fairness, the corrections should be mild and reasonable. It's always best to make the transition from mild corrections to firmer corrections gradual and progressive, so as not to shock or frighten the dog. Some collars will correct with more intensity than others, i.e. prong as opposed to buckle or flat, but that's primarily a matter of technique and learning not to over-do it.

The corrective action from leash to collar is a quick, decisive "snap and release" generated from the elbow and/or the wrist. It is *not* a pulling or restraining technique. As quickly as it happens, it is

also over. The point is just to break the dog's focus from the distraction, allowing a split second to re-direct her toward you. Steadily "pulling" on the collar will never get her attention to shift to you. Constant tension on collar and leash have other bad side-effects as well:

1. "Restraint" doesn't teach the dog. It only frustrates the dog in his desire to achieve his goal. If the dog's *mind* isn't drawn away from whatever he's fixated on, then the frustration can easily increase and intensify. The dog must learn to accept a relaxed collar, demonstrating calm acceptance of your lead.

2. It's the quickest way to do major damage to his neck, windpipe, vertebrae, esophagus, etc.

3. The dog's neck can easily become numb to a correction. Constantly having a collar tightened around her neck will eventually deaden the nerves.

With a collar check, the angle or *direction* of the correction is very important. "Check" the collar in the direction you want the dog to move. The correction should succeed in getting the dog back into proper position. If the dog is pulling ahead, pop straight *back*. If the dog is pulling to the *left*, pop to the *right* to get her back into position. If the dog is refusing to "Sit," angle the collar check *down and back* so her rear end winds up on the ground.

Once the correction is completed, immediately *release* the tension. This is similar to the directive of "not pulling". I've had students who learned how to make a decisive "snap" on the collar but then didn't release quickly enough. The correction shouldn't seem to be ongoing to your dog. Rather, make it appropriately timed, effective and—above all—brief.

Practice your technique and use just the right amount of strength for your particular dog's size, temperament, mood and the immediate situation. The idea is to get the dog's attention with just one or two quick jerks, thus avoiding having to check the collar repeatedly for the same offense.

• Level Two Correction: "Scruff" Discipline •

A dog's "scruff" area is the pelt/hair located directly behind the head, around the neck and above the shoulders. When dogs interact with one another, it is common to see much attention directed at each other's scruff areas. Mother dogs carry their pups by the scruff as well. Since it is such an observable target for communication and interaction between dogs, it makes sense to incorporate it into a form of correction.

There are several ways to deliver a scruff correction. Which one to use will be determined by the command in question and the situation. *None* of the following techniques inflict any discomfort or pain on the dog but, because physical *touch* is involved, all are felt more deeply *psychologically* than a Level One correction. Scruff corrections are done with the hands. There are many reasons why scruff corrections are critical to developing respect:

1. Dogs invariably become what is called "collar savvy". This means they often behave beautifully when the leash and training collar are on. However, when one or both come off the dogs can often ignore you. Scruff corrections address this phenomenon.

2. Because scruff corrections are a hands-on technique the dog experiences them on a more primal level, and he begins to focus less on the collar and leash. You are now demonstrating leadership based on mental strength, not on an extraneous device the dog might be wearing.

3. Scruff corrections directly simulate canine discipline, just like a mother dog or a leader within a pack. Hence, they are more immediately understandable to the dog. It's his language being spoken.

4. As a pup develops and her personality begins to mature, there will invariably be situations where she will simply defy you. (Often this begins to be evident at the onset of adolescence — 6 months to 2 years.) Dogs react to and with their environment. Depending on the situation, when a dog repeatedly refuses to obey the remedy is not to continue jerking a collar. The risk of inflicting damage on the dog's neck is too great, let alone having the situation dissolve into utter frustration — on both sides. For times like these, scruff corrections can help get the dog's attention back on track.

A dog's reaction to a scruff correction can vary widely, being primarily based on certain pre-existing issues:

1. Does the dog have a very confident and outgoing personality, or is he generally timid and insecure? Knowing a dog's temperament is essential so the correction isn't underdone or overdone. For bigger dogs, more rambunctious and/or outgoing personalities, expect to have to be more convincing both in technique and "drama". On the reverse, tone it down considerably for a timid fellow.

2. Have the mixed messages (passive communication) been going on for so long that the dog solidly believes she's in charge, or at least that you're a "nobody" in rank? In these situations it's not unusual for a dog to misunderstand the correction. If you think this is the case, go back to basics with proper passive messaging and train *yourself* better before asking your dog to view you as the legitimate leader. It's never pleasant to find yourself in a situation where the dog is telling you *you're* out of line.

3. Has the technique been done properly, making sure your hand is placed correctly to avoid hurting the dog? Occasionally owners have inadvertently grabbed a portion of a dog's ear along with the scruff — this is quite painful and invariably will result in a lot of squealing or worse. The point, as with all the corrections, is not to hurt the dog. Pain can develop into fear, not respect.

Assuming that all the above items are in order (i.e. the dog isn't confused, your technique is good, and the dog's confidence is moderate to high) dogs still have often been known to squawk, yip or otherwise complain when being scruffed. Getting alarmed isn't necessary. Dogs vocalize considerably when playing and interacting. Rarely does the noise level indicate that someone is actually injured. Some typically "noisy" breeds are German Shepherds, Huskies and Malamutes, Hounds, and Terriers. On the opposite end, I've almost never heard a Labrador Retriever make a peep when being scruffed.

The following "scruff" corrections are in order of increasing intensity. Selecting the right one to use is made on a situation-by-situation basis.

Tag This can be done to rebuff an overly exuberant animal who is invading your personal space (passive message) in a disrespectful manner, including jumping on you. The technique is meant to simulate a "mouth tag" that dogs use on one another. It's usually a preliminary warning. Extend the fingers straight out, stiffening the entire hand. Jab quickly at the dog, "tagging" him around the scruff and firmly pushing him off. Tell him **"No"** as you do so. It may have to be done more than once until the dog stops. Large dogs will require the entire hand, whereas little dogs can be done with only two or three fingers. Do not be stooping or bending over more than is absolutely necessary to deliver the correction. Stand back up as quickly as possible once you're done. It should be noted, though, that rambunctious behavior can often be subdued passively (Chapters 2 and 3).

Scruff Hold Grab scruff directly under the dog's lower jaw or chin and hold firmly, asserting a direct stare. Do not put your face right in front of the dog's! The Scruff Hold is most often and appropriately done with a dog who is mouthy or just sassy. No shaking is involved. Eye contact from you serves to heighten the dominance effect (Chapter 3). Firmly tell the dog or pup **"No"**, then pause until you see the face relax, indicating a change in mood from assertive to passive. As you slowly release, the dog should do nothing, or passively lick your hand. Offer praise for his changed mood.

Scruff Shake This is the most common correction in this category. Grab the dog's pelt firmly right behind the ears on the back of the neck and give 2-3 quick shakes back and forth. Tell the dog firmly **"No"**, at the same time. Do not lift the dog off the ground. Again, watch the dog's reaction after you let go. There should be some indications of submission and passivity.

Side-to-Side Scruff Grab the dog with both hands, one on either side of the neck, about halfway down. Some shaking is involved in this as well. This technique, as the Scruff Hold above, allows for direct eye contact as well as effectively keeping your hands in the clear. Consider using this for dogs who throw tantrums, pitch themselves onto the ground or flail about. It allows the handler to "right" the dog back into a sitting position where control can be regained.

Scruff Pull Use this in certain situations where the dog repeatedly refuses to stay put. A relatively advanced reprimand, be sure you've done sufficient "on-leash" work before challenging the dog in more open settings. Typically used for long distance or "blind" stays, when there's a much higher danger potential for violating the command. This correction involves getting hold of the dog's scruff (as opposed to just grabbing a leash) and returning abruptly to the original spot with him. As with all the corrections, telling the dog "**No**" while you're doing this is important.

Scruff "Down" As the name implies, there's very limited use for this correction. Like the "scruff pull", this is used in an advanced situation. There must be no doubt that the dog understands the "Down" command and has demonstrated a high level of overall responsiveness. The technique is to grab scruff and get the dog quickly over into the Down position, saying "**No**" as you do so. The dog may submit by rolling onto his side—a common reaction. Once you sense he's relaxed, cautiously release your grip, sincerely praising the dog and saying "Good Down". Stand up slowly, but don't pet the dog or allow him to get back up for at least several seconds.

Once again a reminder about "correction protocol": start with the least forceful corrections needed to get the desired response. Be prepared to use up to two or three tries in any given situation before increasing the intensity of the correction. Example: While out walking with Rover, he sees two dogs across the street. His distraction increases as you get nearer the two dogs. You give up to three firm leash corrections, saying **"No"**, attempting to redirect his attention. He remains distracted; it's getting worse. Your next correction might be a "tag" (even a couple of them) then ultimately a "scruff shake" if absolutely necessary. Side note to this: stopping and putting Rover into a Sit/Stay would also seem appropriate to constructively focus his mind on something else.

▪ Level Three Correction: Side or Alpha Roll ▪

This correction mimics a mother pinning a pup to the ground with either her paw or her mouth. The side roll can also be observed occasionally when dogs greet one another. It's common to see a younger, more timid dog drop and roll onto his *side*, possibly even displaying the genital area. It's typically a sign of immaturity, lack of social confidence, or simply a more submissive temperament. The subordinate dog displays a compromising, vulnerable position in order to acknowledge the higher rank and authority of the other animal.

More than any other training technique, this correction evokes strong emotions and opinions both for and against its use. Done improperly, for the wrong reason, or without control and judgment it can lead to physical and/or psychological injury. However, as with all the techniques discussed in the preceding pages this, too, is an observable behavior/ritual between dogs. As human "outsiders", the most critical points to be aware of are *why*, *when*, and *how* it is done. We must use sound judgment, discretion and self-control in situations where this technique might be called into use, *if at all*.

As mentioned earlier in this chapter, encounters between dogs are ritualized for the purpose of avoiding serious conflict. This particular behavior (side roll) is sometimes the final attempt to defuse a potentially volatile or even lethal situation. *Why* it is done, then is basically to appease the more dominant animal. *When* it is done can be either during an initial encounter, during a playful romp with two dogs of equal rank, or with a mother dog sternly reprimanding a pup. Lastly but less common is the seriously aggressive move of a dominant alpha dog against a challenger. *How* it is done depends on the first two issues, the "why" and the "when". If the encounter holds moderate to low volatility, then the behavior is typically volunteered by the more submissive dog. If, on the other hand, the encounter is more intense, possibly holding high danger potential or a "face-off", then the take-down will be more aggressive and abrupt in nature. One dog, essentially, is forced to submit, something like a wrestling match.

What it is *not*: gently rolling the dog onto his back, rubbing the belly and soothing the dog; holding the dog upside down in your arms, again soothing and restraining the dog; holding the dog aggressively on his *back* with the legs loose and pointing up towards you.

This is not a correction to take lightly, and is certainly an advanced technique in any training program. I actually forbid its use with my students until training has progressed to an advanced degree. A dog must demonstrate good responsiveness to commands in a variety of situations and locations. Further, both participants (dog and human) must have a solid understanding about rank and authority, stemming from weeks of practicing proper passive messages as well. Only then can a fair judgment be made about whether or not this correction is *reasonable* and *necessary*. In a nutshell, the better the communication is on all levels, the less likely it is that a situation would degenerate into one where this correction is needed.

Too many injuries, both to dogs and people, have arisen because of poor judgment, improper execution and/or application of this technique. Then there are also the potential emotional injuries. It's quite likely that herein lies much of the controversy. Throughout, it has been my intent to explain that "corrections" by themselves are not the way to communicate leadership, nor are they the way to reach the highest rung of the social ladder. In fact, where there is no relationship built on mutual trust and respect, this particular technique can easily do far more damage than good. This is certainly not a correction to just "try out" on the dog to see what happens, nor is it one to throw around because you've had a rough day at the office. If there's any uncertainty, it's always best to avoid this.

The most common reason why this technique might be called in is based on the *danger potential (serious) of the immediate situation*. This may involve another animal, a human, or simply danger to the dog itself. Besides that, there is also a standard

warning protocol to be followed. The dog should have been told *at least* two times (with lesser corrections) to cease the behavior in question.

Always remember that there are many ways to stop bad behavior or defuse a situation with a dog. This technique should be an absolute *last resort*. If an owner seriously feels he might need to use this correction, they should first seek professional guidance and instruction.

CHAPTER 5

BASIC OBEDIENCE

▪CONSTRUCTIVE MENTAL EXERCISES▪

▪ ELLIE ▪

Photograph Author's collection

Teaching commands to dogs is more about *our* expectations than theirs. If we wish to have a "peaceable kingdom" so to speak, then dogs should be taught manners and controlled behavior to allow us to live together. It's also for reasons of

safety. Most of my students live in urban settings. The dangers inherent in city life are out of the realm of the dog's consciousness. However, we thoroughly understand the need for the dog to *Come* and *Stay* on busy streets and sidewalks. (And, by the way, country dogs aren't free from danger—the dangers are just different.) Lastly, teaching commands to dogs equates with mental gymnastics. It gives their minds something constructive and logical to do. While this may sound odd, the fact is that many dogs seem to simply calm down when their owners keep them busy with physical and mental "tasks" to pass the day. They have a sense of belonging and of value in their pack role.

When looking at the task of teaching commands, it may seem a little overwhelming. If, however, one goes about it in a logical progression, one command building on another, it becomes more achievable. The old saying, learn to walk before you run, is true with dog training as well. This does not mean that one command should be totally mastered before starting the next. Rather, the *order* that the commands will be presented is deliberate to get the dog's needs met as quickly as possible. For instance, since physical needs are initially more critical than psychological needs, "Heel" is presented first so an owner can immediately begin to constructively exercise the dog.

With each command, an explanation of the benefits and/or reasons behind it will be given. Many commands actually do simulate behaviors seen in dog and daily pack behavior. If pertinent, *your* conduct and body language as it pertains to the exercise will be discussed. This is critical because how the dog perceives you has much to do with the level of cooperation and performance. Tips will be given on how to handle the leash for maximum efficiency as well as how to balance enthusiasm, praise and positive reinforcement with the occasional correction.

▪ Timing is Everything ▪

There are two aspects relating to "timing" that should be mentioned at this point in how they relate to teaching. The first is that a response by the owner/trainer needs to be done in a *timely* fashion. Seconds are precious, and the quicker the handler can react when observing unwanted behavior, the better. In most situations, in fact, the decision to correct and redirect is made and acted on *before* there is even any blatant manifestation of wrongdoing. Corrections and/or redirections are most effective (and generally require considerably less drama) when they are applied at the moment when *one first notices that the dog's attention is wandering.* For example, take a typical walk through the neighborhood. A dog sees another dog a block away and begins to whine excitedly. Signs of anticipation are a lifted tail, ears shifting forward and muscles becoming stiff. *This* would be the best and easiest time to offer a redirect, rather than waiting until you are passing the other dog, and suddenly find yourself dealing with an actual lunge, instead of just whining. Think of the "signals" a dog sends as parts of a *sentence*. The change in eye direction,

ear position, muscle rigidity, tail lift, whining, etc., are all parts of this "sentence". The *physical* manifestation seen as a result of the "sentence"—lunging, jumping, snarling—would then be the *punctuation mark* at the end. The time to modify the sentence is when you can see the direction it's heading, *not* once you hit the punctuation mark. Of course, this all means getting more fluent in "dog speak", as sometimes there isn't much time between the signals and the final reaction. Practice and attentiveness, however, will make you more efficient. The quicker you react, the less dramatic your response will need to be.

"Timing" also means effectively linking words with actions in the dog's mind. Some words (primarily commands, but also words used for praise and encouragement) will carry a *positive* association for the dog. Others words (primarily <u>No</u>) will carry a *negative* association. Your voice, essentially, becomes the "event marker", as opposed to, say, a clicker tool. An "event marker" serves to pinpoint with laser accuracy exactly *what* it is the dog did that was either "good" or "bad". When working with a leash, it is essential to begin associating leash corrections with the word <u>No</u>, thus developing a mild negative association in the dog's mind with these two behaviors on your part. Do not associate *command words* with something negative. The dog should never feel threatened by "Heel", "Sit", "Stay", or any of the other commands you may choose.

This separation of "positive" and "negative" can be done relatively easily, if you remember **not** to say command words when pulling on the leash. Here's how it works in the dog's mind:

1. Leash correction is unpleasant.

2. Sounds heard simultaneously with correction are also associated with unpleasantness.

3. Eventually the sounds alone ("No!" is a negative "event marker") are sufficient to get the same result even without pulling on the leash.

In practice, this boils down to *saying No when giving a correction.* Just as importantly, *don't say a command word when giving a correction.* Timing is everything.

Words are used in training because it aids both participants (dog and owner) to make sense out of what is happening. However, understand that words have absolutely no inherent meaning to the dog until we apply them. A word, to a dog, is simply a noise. If we wish to have the dog "understand" that word, then it needs to be heard consistently by the dog in a deliberate way, associated directly with a particular action. Except for "Stay", a dog will associate the word (command) chosen with a particular *action.* For instance, "Heel" is the *action of walking beside you.* "Come" is the *physical approach with a forward facing finish.* "Sit" is the *action of bending the hips to the point that the hind end touches ground.* Owners must grasp this concept so they can appreciate the dog's perspective *and* learn to time positive and negative reinforcers at the appropriate moment.

Lastly, the beginning stage of training is referred to as the "learning" phase. Corrections during this phase should be mild, focusing on learning and developing trust more than anything else. Using too many corrections, or ones that are too harsh in the beginning, can add unnecessary stress to the dog when she is trying to make sense out of these noises (commands) you are making and what is expected of her. If it's necessary to guide the dog now and then for reasons of safety, pressure can be applied to the collar. But it should not be relied upon as the primary way to control the exercise or the dog at this stage. Once the owner is sure the dog thoroughly understands what she is being told to do, then corrections become more reasonable and fair.

• HEEL •

Equipment needed will be a 4'-6' leather or nylon leash, whichever you prefer. Select your collar of choice, based on information offered in Chapter 4. If the choice to use a metal pinch collar or a Triple Crown collar has been made, the dog needs to have been introduced to the collar 2-5 days *prior*. This means he should have been allowed to simply wear it around the house during daily activities in a non-threatening atmosphere. Since these collars are more abrupt than others, it's important to present a broader perspective to the dog, rather than limiting the collar solely to "training" time.

Hopefully, the physical benefits of Heeling are obvious. It allows for controlled, continuous exercise with the added pleasure of not being dragged down the street or tripped by a dog who darts back and forth across the owner's path. It also fits nicely into the category of *mental* exercise as well, because the rules associated with Heeling require attentiveness and listening skills to be fine-tuned. Heeling with your dog is a brisk, purposeful activity that simulates pack movement. There is a direction, a steady pace and a goal, as opposed to the lazy "Sunday stroll" approach where no one is really paying attention to much of anything—at least not for more than 3 seconds at a time. When packs are on the move or on a hunt, there is little time for amusement on the side. Energies are focused on getting to the "finish line" as quickly as possible. As the appointed "leader" of the Heeling expedition, your body language should be one of calm confidence. Standing tall with relaxed arms and shoulders tells the dog you are sure of yourself and the goal. Rigid, stiff or tense limbs indicate the reverse. Look the part and be ready to encourage the dog to follow you.

Stand with the dog on your left side. If you can, guide him into a sitting position with his head up. Hold leash in **both** hands. Keep arms straight at the sides—do not bend the elbows. Place your left hand on the leash, palm facing back in a natural grip. Grip the leash *just far enough away from the clasp so that the collar is **relaxed**.* The leash clasp should just rest gently on the dog's shoulder blades. The spot where the left hand holds the leash will be referred to as the *control point*. Once you've determined its location, commit it to memory and grab the leash there consistently. The

proper position of Prong Collar for Heeling exercise

Photography: Robert Neary

only reason to change the control point would be if you have a growing puppy.

The control point is critical for effective Heeling and quick, efficient corrections. Here's what may happen with improperly placed control points:

1. Too close and the collar begins to tighten or retract. The dog is now simply being *restrained* which ultimately leads to frustration and/or potential injury. He will also have more of a tendency to resist Heeling because he associates the activity with these unpleasant sensations.

2. Too close and it's hard for the dog to understand exactly where you want him to be. The correct "Heeling" location, as far as the dog is concerned, should be where there's no neck discomfort at all. That's an impossible concept to teach the dog if the entire activity is uncomfortable.

3. When a collar is continuously retracted, it is no longer effective as a "teaching" tool. The dog may easily become numb or oblivious to the sensation. Training collars must be *relaxed* in order to efficiently and properly execute the "snap and release" technique.

rear view: proper Prong Collar position for Heeling exercise

Photography: Robert Neary

There are also hazards to having the control point too far away:

1. Too far back and the dog can wander out of position before he feels tension.

2. Too far back and the corrections become weakened. Having to turn your body and/or use your shoulder during the correction shouldn't be necessary. A quick snap from the elbow down is best. (This will become important further into the training.)

3. Too far back can leave a section of dangling leash in front of the dog's face. That's quite a temptation for some frisky personalities. Don't encourage the Heeling exercise to turn into a tug-of-war game.

Choose a location that is familiar and essentially free from distractions. Inside the house is perfectly acceptable to start. A "Heeling course" should be routine and repetitive as well as familiar. This often helps dogs pick up on the patterned nature of the exercise.

If all is in order, pick a point approximately 20 feet away. Cheerfully give the command "Heel" and begin walking at a moderate pace straight ahead. Encourage the dog as you walk, punctuating your speech with lots of enthusiasm and a positive attitude. This is crucial as dogs respond to cheerfulness, eagerness and zeal. Do what you can to get him to *look up* at you frequently. Let him know when he's doing it right. When the 20-foot mark has been reached, stop and take a short break (5-10 seconds). Give plenty of enthusiastic praise, check to make sure the control point is still correct and your arms are relaxed, then start up again. Cover the course back and forth or around a ring for about 10 minutes at a time for very young puppies (10-16 weeks) or up to 15 minutes for somewhat older puppies or dogs. Continue to stop frequently, every 20 feet or so, to break up the course. As the two of you become more proficient at this, gradually move outside to more challenging areas and slowly increase the overall practice time as well.

Choke Chain: proper position for a "left heeling" dog

Photography: Robert Neary

The basic rules for Heeling are as follows:

- Keep the dog in line with you. (Imagine a line running across the end of your toes and keep the dog *behind* it.) Some mild leash corrections in the beginning may be needed to enforce this.

- Don't inadvertently jerk on the collar when you start up. I've had students do this occasionally (it may be a nervous reaction) and it seems to startle the dog. There's no reason for it. To the dog, he feels as though he's getting corrected, but "for what" he's not sure. It can create a nervous, resistant dog. It's especially important to watch out for this if you're using a pinch collar or a Triple Crown Collar.

- Discourage wandering to the sides or serious lagging behind. Keep up the enthusiasm, encouraging the dog to stay focused primarily on *you*.

- Discourage sniffing when heeling. Once the dog's nose hits the ground, at least half of her attentiveness is lost.

- Keep in mind to stop frequently, even if the dog seems do be doing fine.

- Discourage constant bathroom breaks. This can develop into the behavior known as *micturition* — scent marking. A dog that is constantly trying to leave his scent over the last dog that went by is very distracted from Heeling. Furthermore, the behavior is often done to establish territories. Since this is functionally impossible with the number of dogs in tight urban areas, it can easily lead to territorial aggressiveness. The solution — allow for potty business *before* the exercise begins, then get down to work.

▪ Common Problems—Suggestions ▪

Heeling sounds quite simple, and often it is. Then again, you may have a real struggle on your hands. This may go back to how recently the collar and leash were introduced to the dog. Has she had enough time to relax about the collar? Even if all the appropriate "warm-up" work has been done, a puppy may still resist. Don't give up. This is where patience, persistence, creativity and perseverance come in. Here are a few tips and suggestions for the "resisters":

1. Select the first session when the puppy seems to be in a relatively calm mood. Do not practice when she's extremely energetic or extremely tired.

2. Practice at first in a quiet place with little to no distractions so you can hope for more attentiveness from the pup. If there's room, inside the house is always best. If you're outside, stay off grass or bark so as not to encourage sniffing.

3. In spite of the pup's antics, try to walk steadily until the 20-foot mark has been reached. Avoid an erratic fast/slow, stop/start kind of pace that will frustrate and confuse her. If nothing else, she will probably begin to respond to the predictability of the course and the exercise.

4. If your dog appears extremely timid, try looking at her more as you move forward. Work more on eye contact and have a very up-beat, enthusiastic attitude. Remember—dogs respond to positive energy.

5. Stick to the course—don't give in too quickly to the pup's antics. In fact, try to be *more* encouraging and enthusiastic to counter-balance resistant behavior. Believe it or not, she is hearing you. A lot of the resistance encountered in the first few Heeling sessions is often due to nerves on the part of the pup. If you experience this, try not to "correct" or "soothe" her. It might make it worse.

6. Try stopping more often. Perhaps every 5-10 feet may work better in the beginning. Having more "breaks" can make it less arduous on both of you.

7. Find a happy medium between being too lenient (simply giving in to an uncooperative dog) and being a "drill sergeant".

8. Keeping the leash relaxed, walk away several feet. Encourage the dog to follow you. If you are successful, slowly continue walking, avoiding collar pressure. Keep encouraging the dog, giving plenty of praise.

9. Lastly, if several days go by (5-7 on average) and you seem to be making no progress, start luring the dog along, a few feet at a time, with a treat in your hand. Keep the lure right in front of the dog's face if necessary. *However,* **do not** give it to her after only a few feet. Go through 3 or 4 walk and stop sequences before handing it over. Refill your hand and try it again. Eventually put all treats away.

• Tantrums •

Emotional outbursts and displays of extreme resistance are relatively unusual. However, if they *do* occur, they are often linked with fatigue, fear or out-and-out defiance. Avoid the "fatigue" factor by not practicing too long (10 minutes at most with little puppies). Avoid the "fear" factor by keeping a positive attitude and trying to keep the corrections to a minimum. The "defiance" factor is a little trickier to handle and may take a bit more creativity — often it can be traced back to weeks of improper *passive* messages (Chapter 3). The most important thing to remember, though, is *not* to immediately stop the exercise because of the tantrum. The dog, in fact, throws a fit *because he wants you to stop what you're doing!* If you give in, then he sees the outburst as a success: hence it will likely happen again and again. It is not recommended an owner get into a physical struggle with their dog at this stage, but neither should they simply give in when the dog says "No!" That would be similar to handing the candy bar to little Johnny when he's screaming on the floor in the check-out line. If you are unfortunate enough to experience a tantrum, stay calm, and keep your wits about you. Do what you can to work *through* it, without losing control of *yourself*.

▪ SIT ▪

This command allows for a pause, setting the dog into an attentive position while he awaits the next directive, or simply to calmly observe the surroundings. It lends itself to nearly any setting, placing the dog in neither a too assertive (a rigid standing position) nor too submissive (lie down) position. It also goes hand in hand with the Heeling exercise, as with each stop, the dog is taught to "Sit".

above and below: "Sit" demonstration, first method

Photography: Robert Neary

Photography: Robert Neary

The following technique works well for dogs up to about 40-45 pounds. Place the leash on the dog, stand beside him and encourage him to look up at you. Place the open left hand, palm forward, directly *behind* the dog to prevent his backing up. With the other hand gently lift his chin/neck up and angle the pressure backwards, aiming for the ground. As the dog's hips start to bend, say the command "Sit". Continue with the motion until the dog is firmly seated beside you. Offer plenty of praise. **Do not** get into the habit of pushing down on the dog's hips. The left hand is placed behind the dog to prevent the dog from moving out of position, *not* to apply pressure.

above: "Sit" demonstration, alternative method

Photography: Robert Neary

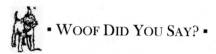

For larger dogs, try this technique. Begin the same way, with the dog on leash beside you. This time, take the left hand and/or forearm and place it behind the dog's back legs at the knee joints. As the command "Sit" is given, apply just enough pressure to get him to bend his knees. Follow through until he is seated beside you. Again, offer plenty of praise.

Either of these techniques allows for mild, non-threatening manipulation that can successfully get the dog to associate the word with the action, "showing" him what you want. Avoid using collar corrections in the beginning, especially if the dog doesn't understand the word.

Once the dog begins to respond to the command without manipulation, transition to using the collar to guide her into position. Slide your hand down the leash, closer to the clasp. This will allow greater strength to be concentrated where you need it. If you have a very small dog, it may be necessary to bend at the knees to accomplish this. With the same angle as suggestion one, pull backwards and down (literally the direction you want the dog to move). Follow through until the dog is seated beside you. It may still be necessary to block the hind-end to prevent backing up.

The most important difference between this last suggestion (collar use) and the previous "manipulation" techniques, is that the owner is now making an actual *correction*. Since pressure is deliberately being applied to the collar, the dog will view this action as a *negative*. Hence, do not use this technique until you are quite sure the dog understands the command. Furthermore, this now falls into the issue of *Timing* as mentioned before. If you need to pull on the collar, don't be saying "Sit", but rather, "**No!**"

The pattern works something likes this:

1. With the leash and collar relaxed, give the command to "Sit", calmly but firmly.

2. Pause 2-3 seconds as you wait for a response.

3. If the dog isn't responding even slightly, deliver a *reasonable* collar jerk/pull as you *simultaneously* say No!

4. Repeat 1 and 2 up to two more times if the dog is particularly stubborn. After that, though, make the decision to follow through by physically manipulating the dog into position. Repeating commands unendingly without any ultimate consequence serves only to teach the dog to ignore you and to frustrate the owner.

Learning the timing issue takes practice and if you're off once in awhile, it's okay. The dog will still learn, especially if you are using a lot of praise and encouragement with the command words. The important thing to remember is to *separate* commands from corrections, making one positive and rewarding and the other, not.

▪ Stay ▪

This is the only command that will *not* be linked in the dog's mind with movement. It is like a little "freeze frame" of whichever position you wish the dog to hold—sit, down or stand. It could, arguably, be the most important command to teach the dog. It develops an attention span in the dog and an ability to focus acutely without being distracted by the surrounding environment. Dogs with highly developed attention spans (those that can hold a "Stay" for long periods of time) seem to be generally calmer than those dogs who can only hold the "Stay" for one or two minutes.

While dogs in the wild probably cannot be observed sitting or standing motionless for really prolonged periods, it is safe to say that with the urban environments many dogs live in today, the "Stay" command could save their lives.

The first "Stay" to teach is the "Sit-Stay". Have the dog's collar and leash on. Stand or sit beside the dog, _holding the leash_. Place the dog away from objects he might try to lean against (furniture, walls, legs). This will encourage more attentiveness and hopefully better posture. Tell the dog to "Sit", guiding him into position if necessary. Then, quickly tell him to "STAY" and focus _all your attention on the dog_.

The rules for this exercise are as follows:

1. No lying down.
2. No standing up.
3. No serious fidgeting or scratching. (Although this may be a stress reaction by the dog, do not allow it to get out of hand.)
4. No leaning against things.

The rules are fairly simple so as to impress on the dog the importance of *not moving*. Do not attempt in the beginning to teach these rules or this command *without* holding a leash. Your reaction time for a correction will be far too slow for it to make sense to the dog and "mark" exactly where the mistake was. If the owner has to walk across a room or farther to get hold of the leash, then the dog has essentially "gotten away" with the "mistake" of moving. As stated in the section on "Timing", effective corrections must be immediately linked with the behavior in question. And the quicker it happens, the quicker the dog learns.

In the beginning, plan to keep the dog in the "Stay" for **two minutes**. This is quite an achievement for some dogs, most puppies and a few people. The two minutes need not be perfect, or uninterrupted, just that you have persisted in the exercise, guiding and encouraging as needed, until the two minutes is up. As with the Heeling exercise, coach and encourage the dog as the exercise is going on. Periodically repeating the command "Stay", in a calm but enthusiastic voice helps attentiveness and word association. I've heard this referred to as "instructive praise". Be patient and diligent. Do not give in or give up too quickly. With calm persistence, in no time, most dogs can achieve the two minute mark with relative ease.

The best approach to this exercise is to naturally incorporate it into other daily activities. I've been know to practice Sit/Stay exercises with dogs in conjunction with household chores such as sorting laundry, unloading dishwashers or cleaning out cupboards. They can also be

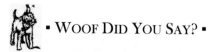

done during that morning cup of coffee, answering of e-mail's or watching your favorite television program. It just requires a bit of your attention be directed at the dog to keep him in position. Try doing them at different times of the day, when energy levels may fluctuate. Always practicing when the dog is already calm is not a realistic approach. Also practice the exercise in a variety of locations, selecting the distraction level that is suited to the dog's skill. Try to fit in as many in a day as your time allows.

As both of you get more adept at this, gradually increase the challenges with longer duration and greater distractions. This exercise has an uncanny ability to calm a dog down in a rapid space of time. While physical exercise is of the utmost importance, there's also nothing like a good long Sit/Stay to calm and settle a wild little puppy. In a pinch, when a long walk is out of the question, these exercises can seem to save the moment.

• Common Problems—Suggestions •

Most of the difficulty with this command comes in when owners let go of the leash and/or can't stay focused on the exercise themselves. Here are the most common difficulties my students tell me about this exercise:

1. **Dog is extremely distracted.** Make sure the first few times you try this, the area selected is relatively quiet and familiar. Also select a time when you can judge the dog's mood is neither too energetic, nor too fatigued.

2. **Dog seems to get a severe and sudden itching attack when the command is given.** Don't over-react too much to this. It is likely a "Calming Signal" (behavior dog performs when under stress). The first few times, calmly coach the dog *through* the itching behavior, making sure that he doesn't break out of position as soon as he's done.

3. **Dog is extremely fidgety and constantly moves and slides around.** Take seriously the suggestion to *hold the leash*. This is really the only way to effectively control the exercise to any reasonable degree. *Not* holding the leash allows for confusion regarding what "Stay" means and how much motion is acceptable.

4. **Dog is constantly trying to lie down.** It may be that the dog is simply too tired. (Pick a better time when he's got more energy.) Then again, it could be a submissive response to the exercise itself. Dogs with very timid personality types can overreact and attempt to appease you with the most dramatic display they can think of. If this happens, do not become frustrated. Do not "hold" the dog up with constant tension on the leash. Also try to avoid repeatedly pulling the dog back up with the leash—this will almost always backfire with timid dogs—the more you "correct" the more submissive the dog becomes. These types of personalities often need more confidence building and enthusiasm. Try shorter lengths of time (maybe 1 minute) in the beginning and/or holding a toy or something above the dog's head to keep his focus on a pleasurable object.

• RECALL •

The benefits of the Recall should speak for themselves. Ever hear of someone who *didn't* care whether their dog came when she was called?? I rest my case. All glibness aside, though, there are profound safety reasons why this command is up there in the top three. From a behavioral standpoint, making sure that the dog understands it is *her* task to come to *you* indicates rank. Having to repeatedly "Go and get the dog" places the owner in a subordinate role. Dogs should follow their owners' lead, not the other way around. The ultimate test is whether a dog will come easily *off-lead* to their owners. That should be the long-term goal.

Depending on an individual dog's temperament, the Recall can be challenging. Some breeds are decidedly independent or aloof. Others are very easily distracted. But even the most cooperative dogs can benefit in their responsiveness to this command if approached in an enthusiastic, positive and realistic manner. Some ground rules are critical for best results.

1. Basic introduction to the recall **must** be done **on-lead**. This isn't just for safety. It is also due to the nature of the command—it should *never* be considered by the dog as optional. Having a leash on allows the owner to reinforce should the dog decide to ignore the command. Always be aware of this when working with the dog. Leaving no "safety net" can undermine authority when it comes to this command. Worse, it can also lead to tragedy.

2. Insist on having the dog's attention. Some of the worst mistakes people make with this (in addition to no leash) are to call the dog when he's loose, running around the backyard, or tearing through the house. In such situations, you are probably the furthest thing from his mind, and in a practical sense, it's arguable whether your voice is even registering with him. The solution is to place the dog into a "Sit/Stay" position so you have his attention.

3. Never come across angry or threatening. Do not bark this command at the dog like he's in trouble. The command word should never be linked with a correction or an unpleasant end. All too often, owners inadvertently associate "Come" with discipline, calling a dog over to point out a transgression that happened in the past. On this same note, do not use "Come" as a diversion to stop unwanted behavior. Your voice can too easily reveal underlying frustration, possibly making the dog suspicious.

4. Be prepared to use *yourself* as the ultimate reward for this command. This means the owner must be genuinely enthusiastic, excited and able to use body language and energy to entice the dog's response. Using treats may initially appear to get a more immediate response, but that often denies a broader perspective and can "sell the dog short", reducing this exercise to nothing less than bribery. I've been known to resort to treats only with completely independent and otherwise unresponsive dogs, and only after several weeks of the other approach.

When beginning this command, you must have made solid progress with the "Stay", being able to get a reliable 2 minutes from your dog. If not, go back and lay the groundwork for that first. After all, if the dog can't be still for more than a few seconds, how will you get his attention to teach this next command? Equipment needed will be a long lead—20 feet is good to start. The procedure is as follows:

1. Attach the 20-foot leash, place dog into a sitting position. Tell her to "Stay". Pause to make sure she is focused, then *slowly* begin to back away. Keep eyes on the dog as you back up. Calmly continue to remind the dog to "Stay". Try to get at least 6 feet away, 10 feet is even better. All the while, repeat "Stay" with good eye contact.

2. Once the designated distance has been reached, pause briefly (5-10 seconds). Do not allow the dog to anticipate and come before the command is given. If this occurs, give the dog a "No!" and return her *rapidly* to the original spot. Repeat Item #1.

3. When ready, say the dog's name and then immediately and with great enthusiasm, offer the command to "Come". Your voice should encourage the dog—the command should appear as a heartfelt invitation.

4. Drawing up of the leash is appropriate, but avoid applying pressure as part of the exercise. The goal is **not** to have to pull the dog in. If positive energy alone sufficiently motivates the dog, then pulling on the collar will only serve to undermine enthusiasm, possibly even making her resistant.

5. Continue to "act out" the part, "rooting" for the dog as she makes her way across.

6. Finish the exercise with the dog sitting in front of you. Immediately offer lavish praise and affection.

Encourage Recall with enthusiastic body language.   Photography: Robert Neary

Finish for the "Recall" command.

Photography: Robert Neary

▪ Common Problems— Suggestions ▪

1. Dog is unresponsive— Several things can be done to help motivate. Try squatting down to the level of the dog. Lowering your "apparent" height makes you appear less dominant and threatening. Some timid personalities may need this to boost confidence. Don't be impatient

for the dog's initial response. Give up to three good, enthusiastic tries. Clap your hands together, pat on your thighs, tap on the floor, anything that gets the dog's curiosity peeked. If possible, pause longer than 5-10 seconds. With some dogs, the longer they're made to wait, the more motivated they are to get back beside you. Try reducing the distance to just a few feet at first. In these situations, try doing a "run-away" game as well, to spark the dog's play-drive. As he starts approaching you, begin backing up rapidly, covering another 10' or more before stopping and letting him catch you. (Once there have been a few successful runs at this, most dogs are quick to respond, as they learn what the "reward" is—lavish affection and praise).

2. Tried all above suggestions, still no response—This is why the 20-foot leash is on. Best suggestion is to give three enthusiastic, sincere attempts to get a response. Finally, resort to the leash. Under these situations, the hard rule is *not* to say "Come" *when you have to snap the leash.* Pause momentarily from all enthusiasm, give a sufficient jerk on the leash with a "No!", then *immediately* relax the collar, returning to an enthusiastic "Come!" with the suggestions from Item #1. The leash jerk needs to have sufficient force to get the dog to snap out of his apparent reverie.

3. Lastly, one may pass a very small food reward to the dog. Do not wave it at the dog from a distance as a bribe. Give a food reward as little as possible, perhaps only 1 time in 5 so as to keep the dog's curiosity peeked. Dogs often work

harder in certain situations in the *hope* of a pay-off. An "every-time" reward often becomes dull and mundane. As his responses improve, switch to praise as the primary reward, using treats less and less.

▪ DOWN ▪

This command, and the body position it creates, indicates submission. Dogs don't just walk up and lie down in front of one another unless they are well-acquainted, or they are trying to convey their subordinate rank. To a great many dogs, this command can create feelings of insecurity, anxiety or even out-and-out defiance. Because of the psychologically weighty nature of the "Down", it's best to present it last. Spend the first two to four weeks of training laying sufficient preliminary groundwork with commands of a less threatening nature to the dog. This will establish your rank of authority, but also help the dog become more willing to trust and cooperate.

Keeping in mind the dog's perspective on "Down", it makes sense to avoid coercing her into position if at all possible. Timid dogs can easily become fearful if this command is presented in too heavy-handed a manner. For the opposite reason, extremely assertive dogs can be just as resistant. With these latter personality types, cooperating for a "lesser" command may be one thing, but offering the most submissive position there is may seem above and beyond the call of duty.

There are many benefits associated with this command. It allows for much longer "Stay" exercises, as the dog is considerably more comfortable than holding a sitting position. Since it also conveys a calmer, more submissive state-of-mind, it lends itself to many situations when one might want the dog to be less rambunctious and playful — large social gatherings for instance, with or without children.

In a concerted attempt to avoid coercion or arousing anxiety in the dog, this is typically the only command that I present with treats. Taking the dog's mind off the psychological nature of the command and directing it onto something enjoyable seems to do the trick in the beginning. Resistance, if any, is reduced to bare minimum, and the dog develops a positive association with the command word itself. As the dog becomes more cooperative, relaxed and trusting about the command, food is gradually reduced and eventually removed completely.

Here's the step-by-step how-to:

1. Place short leash on the dog and put her into a Sit/Stay position.

2. Stand, pull up a chair, or squat beside the dog. Try to *avoid sitting on the floor* next to the dog, even if you have a small breed. The reason is that you want to be *above* the dog's eye level if at all possible. It may appear minor to us, but getting the dog used to going "Down" when you are in a "dominant" posture beside her is an important psychological aspect of this exercise. It is not recommended you "play this up" by staring or being

threatening to the dog. Simply try to avoid being too cozy in the beginning. I had an elderly woman as a student once who trained "Down" up on her bed with her Shih Tzu during snuggling time. She claimed great success (no big surprise!) but was completely unable to reproduce the behavior anywhere else!

3. Use one hand to hold leash, the other to handle the treats. Do not switch back and forth, as one hand should be clear of the smell of food.

4. Hold **two** very small treats or kibbles in your hand: one firmly gripped between thumb and first two fingers, the other being held, hidden, behind the fourth and fifth fingers.

5. Without any ceremony, present the treat hand to the dog, placing your hand *right in front of her face*. The idea is to have the dog's *full* attention, without causing her to feel she needs to snap at your hand to get the food. If the hand is right against her mouth, she is more likely to lick or even nibble a little at the food. Treats held just beyond reach excite more anxiety and curiosity, causing many dogs to snap at the food and/or get up out of the Sit/Stay.

6. Encourage the dog to focus intently on the food, saying things such as "Good girl", "That's right", and so on.

7. Wait a few seconds, making sure the dog is completely engrossed by the food, then begin to *slowly* lower your hand in a straight line towards the ground, aiming for her front paws. Continue, all the while encouraging the dog to

remain focused on the food. **Do not apply pressure to the collar.**

8. Once your hand reaches the floor, pause again a few seconds—hopefully the dog hasn't lost interest. Now begin the slow pull *away* from her, along the floor. The actual movement of your hand will resemble an "L".

9. It is critical that the dog *not* be allowed to break out of the "Sit/Stay" position. This requires fast reaction time for the owner, should her rear end begin to rise in an attempt to get the slowly retreating food. If this occurs, use the leash to quickly reassert the Sit/Stay. Start from Item #4 again.

10. If all goes well, the dog will figure out quickly that the only path to get the food is into a prone position. *As you see this happening,* that is the appropriate moment to suddenly offer the command "Down" (word association with the motion) releasing the treat the very moment the dog has completed the action and her belly is on the ground.

Hold dog's attention with food. Show the treat to the dog.
Photography: Robert Neary

Release treat as soon as dog is flat.
Photography: Robert Neary

11. Lastly, but very importantly, get the treat hand away from the dog's face, placing it quickly

behind your back. Leaving your hand (with the second treat still in it) next to her mouth, will only increase her curiosity and desire to get at it.

12. Calmly praise the dog, watching and monitoring to make sure she doesn't just "swallow and run". This means keeping the other hand *gently* placed (do not *hold* the dog down) over the dog's shoulders. She must not be allowed to abruptly push up out of position, just because she's finished eating the treat. Calmly assert the "Stay" at this point, making sure she will remain in position for 10-15 seconds.

13. If you have succeeded so far, bring back your hand with the other treat. Start again in front of the dog's face, making sure she knows you have more food. Reverse the movement, slowly lifting the food straight *"Up"* to get the dog to return to a sitting position. Release the second treat and calmly praise again.

This is pretty straight forward and I've had the best success with the majority of dogs using this approach. The best thing about it is that, with most cases, the owner doesn't have to lay a finger on the dog—the position is *offered* by the dog in order to get the food. Thus, since there is no coercion or force used, there's no reason for the dog to feel any threat associated with the action. "Down" becomes a *pleasant* experience more than a demonstration of rank.

Sometimes creativity is needed on the selection of the "treat". Some dogs are happy with any old biscuit, others are more selective. I've used very small tidbits of cheese, freeze-dried sheep's liver, cold cuts, hot dogs, or bits of leftover meat. One Shih Tzu had such gourmet tastes he would cooperate only for fresh garlic bread! Then again, even if the food is right, initially there is bound to be some degree of confusion on the part of the dog. How is she supposed to know right away *how* to get the treat? This only happens through calm persistence, trial and error, and having a few successes until the dog begins to figure out the game. Don't get impatient. It often takes 6-10 solid successes, one right after the other, before it seems to click.

When presenting this command, I lay out an approach that allows for well over 100 repetitions of this over the course of just a few days: 12-15 sequences at a time, 2-3 times every day usually starts to have a positive impact on the dog. Once in awhile a dog seems to "get it" very quickly, but that's not necessarily the norm. As you are building up the dog's level of cooperativeness and understanding with this, stick with the food reinforcement for the first week, *if* you have been practicing regularly. On the other hand, if practice is only happening once every three days, expect this to take a very long time.

• Common Problems—Suggestions •

1. **Dog completely disinterested in the food.** Since all dogs need to eat, try doing the exercise an hour or so before mealtime, so you know the appetite is good. Again, play around with what is being used to lure the dog. Creativity is good here, as long as it's not terribly unhealthy — one student wanted to use pieces of a Halloween cookie.

2. **Dog is nervous and distracted.** Find a place to do this where the dog feels secure. Perhaps on his own bed is a good start. With timid dogs, use as little force as possible, being sure not to unconsciously pull on the leash/collar to get the dog into position. This can set the dog way back on his willingness to give in.

3. **Tried everything, still no success.** *Patience is very important.* If the sequences have been presented diligently for more than four days with not a single success, both dog and owner are likely getting weary of the exercise. It may now be time for some gentle manipulation. Following the guidelines above, **and** being sure the dog is hungry, follow the steps through to Item #7. At this point, while the dog is still focused primarily on the treat, use the *other* hand to quickly come around behind and push the dog into position at the shoulders. This takes some quick action, because the dog shouldn't notice the other hand approaching. Apply pressure *at an angle* (not straight down) trying to get the dog slightly off-balance and over into a relaxed "Down" position. The command word is said *as the owner is pressing the dog into position.* Praise is offered immediately once the dog is "Down", as well as giving him the food. Continue to leave your hand over the shoulders to follow-through with a "Stay" for several seconds.

4. **Another technique** is to gently pull the front legs forward, but only as far as necessary until the dog completes the action himself, finishing the "Down" on his own.

With Suggestions 3 or 4 (manipulation techniques) make sure the force is sufficient to get the job done, but not so much as to frighten the dog or come across as a disciplinary move on your part. Since the dog will be in a submissive position at the end, it's important to leave him be at that point, just calmly reinforcing the "Stay". Avoid petting and stroking. Timid dogs might translate this as a reinforcement for a possibly nervous or apprehensive state-of-mind. Assertive dogs might translate the extra stimulation as an excuse to pop up out of position.

• Charting Progress •

When teaching each new command, keep the sessions relatively short. 10-12 minutes on any particular one (Heeling might be longer to meet the exercise needs of the dog) should be sufficient, encouraging you to come back and repeat it 2-3 times throughout the day. Do not get impatient with the dog. Rather, keep a positive, enthusiastic attitude and be open to the messages that she might send you. Read the dog's body language as you train. Modify the approach to enhance the dog's strengths, as well as helping her work through her weaknesses. Training is one of the single best ways to get to know your dog, and to bond constructively with her. Try never to look at training as a "chore". If you have a positive attitude, so will the dog. I've had many students tell me how excited their dogs get when they see the training collars come out.

Present the commands one at a time, allowing for a reasonable level of competence with one before adding the next. Present them in the order given, a few days to a week or more apart, especially if working with a young puppy. The commands are meant to build on one another in a cumulative manner. While it isn't necessary to demonstrate perfection with one exercise before starting the next, some commands ("Stay" for instance) are more foundational in nature than some others. This means that working on the dog's attention span in general will certainly improve his performance in all other respects.

Do not look for solid, lasting results to happen immediately. Like all things in life, change takes time. The longer an owner has delayed training, and/or the more deeply imbedded the bad habits, the more patient and calmly persistent the training must be. The whole adolescent phase can also slow progress. Many, many people have thought they had a behavior licked, only to have it resurface when their dog hit adolescence!

It is too subjective an issue to project time frames on dog progress. Many students notice dramatic improvement in their dog after just one week (and are then greeted with an episode of "Spontaneous Recovery"—sudden but typically short-lived reemergence of a behavior). Then again, there are those who struggle for weeks or months before the pay-off suddenly becomes obvious. This is an aspect of training that many people find difficult to handle. Perhaps it stems from our culture that sells and advocates "instant gratification". The understanding

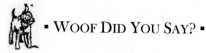

you have with your dog, however, doesn't fit into this category. The best relationships are those that develop over time, where the cornerstones are patience and understanding.

Through all things, try as best you can to demonstrate and exhibit *consistency* in handling the dog. This alone is probably the biggest problem in training and communication. People simply get worn down, or the unpredictability of life intrudes on their best intentions. Also, by our very nature, humans are largely inconsistent—and I include myself in this statement. Because of our emotions and senses of humor, we often "let slide" things that we ought not to. Thankfully, however, one need not be 100% on any of these issues to still have a great relationship with and/or have a well-behaved dog. Recognizing where the weaknesses are, and committing to work for improvement, is part of the process.

Lastly, do not make the mistake of thinking of an obedient dog as a "done deal". Because a dog is a living creature, with her own set of needs, wishes and drives, maintaining an obedient dog should always be seen as a *work in progress*. A trained dog is not like a sculpture that, when completed, can be set on a shelf for all to admire. After the initial "learning phase" has been successfully completed, all that is generally required is steady, consistent reinforcement. But, it does have to be steady and consistent. One is not just a leader for a few short weeks, but a leader for a lifetime.

CHAPTER 6

INTERMEDIATE AND
ADVANCED OBEDIENCE
▪ MOVING BEYOND LEASHES ▪

▪ SYDNEY & EMMA ▪

Photo courtesy Author's collection

Once a dog has learned what a command means and is performing satisfactorily in a familiar environment, the next phase is to present challenges to him that test his ability to rise above distractions, whatever they may be, and to trust completely in the decisions of the leader. This usually

involves getting the dog out of his "comfort zone" and gradually increasing the distractions. It also deals directly with social skills, making sure the dog is confident and relaxed no matter where he may find himself.

Socialization of a dog is an integral part of overall reliability with obedience. Practicing regularly with a dog is important, but if it's always in the same location or environment it becomes stagnant and unrealistic. This is sometimes the case with a group class as well. An owner may assume that their dog is learning how to interact with other dogs simply because they attend class every week. But, if the in between time doesn't allow for more varied and natural dog encounters, then all a dog learns is how to get along with her familiar "classmates".

Socialization, even more than "playing nice" with other dogs, has to do with confidence and good manners in the human world. A dog doesn't just wake up one morning and find himself ready to face life's challenges. If one wishes their dog to behave well in a variety of settings, then practices should be conducted purposefully in those specific settings, helping the dog become familiar and relaxed. It is, thus, incumbent on the owner to commit to taking the dog out regularly for the sole purpose of enhancing social skills.

Furthermore, with intermediate and advanced exercises, there is a slow but deliberate withdrawal (in a figurative sense) from regularly "directing" the dog while still being ready on a moment's notice to

respond and guide if needed. The goal is to encourage the dog to demonstrate "on his own" what he has learned. Ideally the dog will use his knowledge to make the correct choices without the owner needing to direct and cue at every move. This "withdrawal" is accomplished over time and done in many ways:

- by expecting good citizen behavior at home, even without his "training collar" being on,
- by not cueing the dog every single time on routine responses,
- by gradually reducing the verbal coaching,
- by removing obvious visible incentives,
- by increasing the physical distance between dog and owner,
- by placing the dog in situations where he is tempted to give in to his natural curiosity, and
- by extending the length of time he is expected to pay attention.

All these approaches encourage the dog to rely more and more on his own memory and knowledge of what is expected of him. This approach also succeeds in building a dog's confidence, as with each success he realizes he can do things properly without the constant presence and guidance of the owner .

The commands will be presented in the same order as the preceding chapter. More suggestions on how to approach each other will be offered, challenging both dog and owner to improve their overall skill. I call the challenges the "3 D's": *duration, distance and distraction.*

For some of the following exercises, a 20-foot leash will be used.

▪ HEELING ▪

INTERMEDIATE LEVEL EXERCISES

▪ Auto-Sit ▪

This exercise encourages the dog to remain attentive and follow-through with a predictable response to a routine situation. It demonstrates a willingness on the part of the dog to share responsibility, demonstrate initiative and remember details without having to be cued for each step. The idea is to have the dog sit of his own volition when a stop is made during the Heeling exercise. The process is simple, and can be attempted once the owner feels that the dog is sufficiently adept at standard Heeling. Furthermore, if an owner has witnessed the dog occasionally sitting on his own at a stop point, then he is likely ready for this.

Another prerequisite to this exercise is making sure the dog has developed a respect for "No!". In other words, the dog must visibly acknowledge this word when he hears it, stopping the behavior in question and redirecting his attention to the owner. If this is not the case, go back and re-read the section on corrections in Chapter 4 where it talks about using the voice. A calm but firm voice serves as an "event marker", getting the dog's full attention.

To teach the Auto-Sit, present the heeling exercise as usual. However, when you stop, say *nothing*

for the first 2-3 seconds. This pause allows the dog the opportunity to demonstrate whether he:

1. has learned the patterned nature of this exercise,
2. is paying full attention to said exercise, and
3. is willing to take the initiative and follow-through on his own.

Hopefully, the dog will rise to the challenge and drop into position, at which point, enthusiastic praise should flow! If, however, 3 seconds comes and goes and nothing is happening, turn, look directly at the dog and give a calm but firm **No** in a low voice. This move on the part of the owner is like calling a bluff in a poker game. If one is relatively sure the dog is conditioned to "Sit", then the **No** serves as a sort of "push" or "reminder", encouraging the dog to demonstrate his knowledge of the exercise. In other words, you have done your part (walk and stop) and know it's the dog's turn to do his part (Sit). This move on the part of the owner encourages the dog to use his own initiative, do his own thinking and *choose* to Sit, rather than waiting to be *told* to do so. Sometimes it takes a couple warning "No's", but most of the time the dog comes through. Again, enthusiastic praise should flow, indicating to the dog exactly what was expected.

If, after two warning "No's" the dog remains standing, offer the "Sit" command, even guiding him into position if needed. Do two or three more rapid walk-stop-sit sequences, giving all the cues. Then try the Auto-Sit again. Eliminating the precise command word from this exercise generally isn't confusing to the dog, especially if he's familiar enough with the pattern. The purpose is to encourage heightened attentiveness and a "team" effort, rather than leaving the burden solely with the owner.

▪ Turns ▪

Some fancy footwork when heeling is always a good idea to add variety and keep the dog's attention focused where it should be—on the one holding the leash. The first ones to try are right pivots and/or turn-abouts. With left-heeling dogs, both of these turns should be away from the animal. Turns should be crisp and smooth. The dog should not be expecting the turn, hence encouraging him to keep focused. Learning to spin or pivot on the ball of your foot as you come around will make the turn more fluid and effortless. It will also make it less noticeable to the dog, again encouraging more attentiveness to detail.

A slightly trickier turn is the left pivot. Here the owner turns abruptly *into and across* the dog's path at a 90-degree angle, then continues on in that direction for several paces. This turn can be used as a secondary corrective technique (other than a collar correction) to keep a dog in proper heeling alignment. Timing is crucial for this technique to be effective. Watch carefully as the dog begins to sneak ahead. When his *shoulders* become even with your *feet*, execute the turn. Pivot and spin quickly on the *left* foot, bringing the *right* leg around the corner *first*. Abruptly bump the dog at his shoulder area, cutting quickly across his path. This will cause him

to instinctively *back up* to get out of the way. The dog will rarely see it coming and, in the process, will rapidly be pushed back into position.

These occasional turns allow for relaxed leashes, relying more on body language and maneuvering to keep the dog in alignment. As a result, the dog, for his part, must learn to keep his eyes on the handler, else he will miss the subtleties of an impending quick pivot.

▪ Location ▪

While this doesn't qualify as another technique, per se, be aware that if the same heeling route is taken with the dog day after day, week after week, the challenges become non-existent. Never assume a dog to be an excellent heeler until you can be sure she will perform as well in a variety of locations. Neighborhood streets are relatively sedate. Try some of the following locations:

1. a playground filled with noisy children
2. a busy commercial area
3. heeling through a crowd of people
4. heeling through a crowd of dogs

The above suggested locations carry a higher intensity of energy, as well as danger potential should the dog perform poorly. Therefore, take the locations progressively, achieving a reasonable level of proficiency before moving to the next.

▪ Pace ▪

On any given walk, deliberately change speed from medium to slow to fast. Switch back and forth without warning to check and monitor the dog's attentiveness. Be prepared to give some verbal and/or collar corrections as needed the first few tries. These variations, like turns, also serve to encourage better eye contact from the dog.

ADVANCED LEVEL EXERCISES

▪Off-Leash Heeling ▪

Getting to this level of reliability with a dog is quite an achievement. Knowing that a dog will remain "at his post" with or without a leash is a testament to serious practice *and* impeccable social confidence. The exercise outlined below is the first step toward unhooking the dog. Understanding that most cities have rigid leash laws, a 20-foot leash will be used to stay safe and not violate any ordinances. How quickly any particular dog can achieve reliability with off-leash Heeling is highly subjective. First, regular Heeling must be very good, requiring very few corrections. Second, social confidence and relaxation in a variety of settings is also important. Thirdly, like most things, overall performance is directly related to how much practice is put in.

The exercise is set up to simulate the absence of a leash. Although a 20- foot leash is attached, it should be extended out behind you and the dog to prevent the possibility of inadvertently creating tension on the collar. Hold the hand loop in the right hand. Keep the left hand *empty.* Begin with the dog sitting attentively at

left heel position. Give the command "Heel" as usual and begin slowly walking in a straight line. Keep eyes on the dog, and encourage the same from him. Calmly coach the dog, using your voice, body language and left arm/hand to act as a focal point. I've been known to pat enthusiastically on my left thigh/hip or snap my fingers to get the dog to look at me. Whistling also can work at times. Walk only a few steps at a time, perhaps 10 feet at most. Stop and immediately direct the dog to "Sit".

beginning position for Off-Leash "Heel" exercises

Photography: Robert Neary

Photography: Robert Neary

This sequence is repeated several times, always keeping the pace slow and even, stopping frequently and calmly encouraging the dog to keep his attention on you. Best times to attempt this are the last 3-5 minutes of a long walk when the dog's exuberance and energy are somewhat abated and controllable. Being in a familiar location also helps, as the dog is less likely to have his curiosity get the better of him.

Occasionally, the dog may test your ability to keep him in position, especially after he's noticed you're not holding a leash. There may very well be a distraction that defeats the dog's ability to focus on you. For times like these, the owner may have to get hold of the dog's scruff to bring him back into position. If this happens, make sure it is as *non-aggressive* as possible. Grabbing abruptly or flashing your hand out, snatching at his pelt is too threatening in this situation. It may make the dog nervous or anxious. Instead, aim to "guide" the dog back into position with the scruff.

Voice control is probably the most important aspect of this exercise, so the owner should have done their homework prior to attempting this, making sure that in most other situations the dog is able to listen and respond to voice directives—both positive and negative. Having to tell the dog "No!" on occasion is not at all unusual for this exercise, especially in the beginning. As you walk forward, watch the dog's position and alignment. If he starts to wander, react immediately with more verbal coaching and encouragement, redirecting his attention back onto you. Sometimes this requires a "No" to be thrown out as well, then quickly follow-through with the redirect and repeating of the command. The point of the exercise is to *deliberately avoid grabbing at the leash* for every false step the dog takes. Rely, instead, on all the other ways you have learned to control and direct the dog.

This exercise may also be done with a remote collar, but I recommend that it *not* be the dog's first introduction to such a training tool.

• STAY •

Intermediate or Advanced levels of the "Stay" command are primarily about the three D's: **d**uration, **d**istance, and **d**istraction level. What separates intermediate from advanced is the degree to which the dog is proficient at any one of them.

Jake

Photograph from Author's collection

• Duration •

From the "Stay" exercises in Chapter 5, gradually but steadily increase the length of time the dog can focus. Building from the initial 2 minute suggestion, add 30 seconds every 2-3 days until the dog can easily sustain a 5-minute Stay. For this particular exercise, it is still recommended to stand close to the dog, holding the leash just in case he attempts to "break". Remember, reaction time is always critical. Learn to guide and refocus the dog at the very moment you can first tell his attention begins to wander. The more timely your response, often the smaller the correction needs to be. Continue to adhere to the rules of no leaning, standing up or lying down.

Many years ago during my apprenticeship for training certification, my employer had a demonstration dog who would hold a Sit/Stay for what seemed like hours, perched on a padded stool in the training room. Business would be conducted around

him, clients could come in and out, dogs and cats could walk by, but this dog would remain focused and attentive. While few people have pursued the "Stay" to this extent, don't underestimate your dog's mental strength. Find and use it! As long as the dog is comfortable in his Stay position, (that is, you're not straining a puppy's joints) who knows how far you might get with this.

▪ Distance ▪

In addition to developing great focal stamina within the dog, teaching her that she can do it "solo" is a great step forward. Ultimately, an owner shouldn't have to stand beside their dog to get the desired results. Gradually backing up and backing away is the next step, developing confidence and reliability within the dog. The rules do not become relaxed, just presenting another way to test the dog's understanding of "Stay".

This exercise is done with the owner holding the end of a 20-foot leash, or with a retractable leash, locked at approximately 15-20 feet. Tempting fate by simply setting the leash on the ground and walking away, or not using one at all is ultimately too risky and possibly a recipe for failure. Too many dogs will quickly notice the loophole and take advantage of it. Even if the location doesn't present any big dangers, at the very least, not holding onto a leash dramatically slows down the reaction time—it takes too long to run after a dog to grab the end of the leash. There is no shame in using that "safety net" until both you and the dog are comfortable with a solid track record of success.

Gaining distance on the "Stay" should be done gradually and progressively. Every few days, another 3-5 feet can be added, making the growing space barely perceptible to the dog. It is strongly recommended that you remain where you and the dog can see one another until a reliable 2-5 minutes can be achieved on a Distance Stay. Here's a typical approach to this exercise:

1. With the 20-foot leash on, place the dog into a Sit/Stay.

2. Slowly back away, feeding the leash out. (Be careful to avoid inadvertently pulling on the collar, possibly confusing the dog.) Keep your eyes focused on the dog. Remind him to "Stay".

3. Slowly continue to retreat, trying to get at least 6 feet away.

4. If the dog successfully handles this initial retreat, begin adding mild distractions. Walk slowly back and forth (towards the dog and away, to the left and to the right) at all times keeping an eye on the dog. Continue to remind him to "Stay" as you do this for a couple of minutes. Try varying your posture at times: standing, sitting, squatting. If at any point the dog gets up and moves, use your voice immediately with a "No!" (marking the event) and react as quickly as you can with a correction. The most important thing is to get him back *as fast as possible* to the spot he was in. Do the exercise again.

For a realistic approach, do this exercise in many different locations, both inside and outside. Routine, daily activities lend themselves to this exercise as well. I've successfully incorporated Distance Stay exercises into household chores—kitchen tidying up, unloading a dishwasher, sorting laundry, making beds, dusting, etc. More than one family member can participate at a time, providing multiple distractions. *However*, do not confuse the dog by allowing two or more people to give simultaneous commands or corrections. As you see the dog improving, keep adding greater distance and longer time.

Lastly, begin relying less and less on a leash. If the dog's performance merits, remove both training collar and leash in some situations. This will help in two very important ways. First, it will develop an understanding in the dog's mind that obedience isn't bound to specific "tools". Second, it will force the owner to practice other methods of controlling the dog should a mistake occur. An owner might find that body language, confident energy and general attention to detail helps immensely to keep the dog in position. It also forces owners to learn good technique and skill with Level Two Scruff Corrections (those that don't depend on a leash) which are detailed in Chapter 4.

▪ Common Problems—Suggestions ▪

The most common problem that people have with this exercise is that the dog keeps moving. Plain and simple. Dogs fidget for many reasons: they're timid and can't stand to be apart from the owner, they are independently-minded and can't be

bothered with it; they're stressed and wiggle around as a way to calm themselves. Occasionally there is even good old-fashioned laziness. With the latter situation, the dogs usually lie down as soon as the opportunity presents itself. If any or all of these things keeps happening, first go back to basic Stay exercises for a few days, rigidly enforcing an upright posture from the dog, coupled with a good long attention span. Then return to the issue of distance. For extreme situations, I've resorted to securing the dog with a short leash to a solid object (furniture leg, cupboard handle, base of a shrub, etc.) to simply prevent her from getting up and walking away or coming towards me. Once you have successfully eliminated the dog's "option" to move around, they tend to settle into the reality of the situation, accepting the exercise and psychologically learning to normalize the issue of your authority over distance.

• Distraction •

This is the last of the "3 D's" with the Stay. This draws directly on the dog's confidence in a variety of locations, as well as social skills. As mentioned earlier, dogs don't just suddenly become able to handle distractions after a certain age. Rather, it is incumbent on the owner to deliberately present varied situations to force the dog to grow and gain confidence with his skills. Obedience is of little practical use if an owner can only rely on the dog to respond from living room to kitchen, when no one else is around.

There are only so many distractions you'll be able to come up with around the house. For a real

challenge, **you must go out.** Here are some suggestions of places to practice with your dog where the distractions are good and socialization can be combined into the exercises:

1. **Retail Stores** Stand out in front near the entrance and practice all the commands. If it's not a food store, they may even allow you inside.

2. **Playgrounds** especially when there are children around. Start slowly, keeping a cautious distance until you sense the dog isn't overwhelmed with the energy or noise level. Once the Stays are going well, gradually increase distance and duration as well. If children want to pet your dog, make sure she is in a Sit/Stay and that *only one child at a time approaches the dog.*

3. **Sporting Events** This implies kid's sports, i.e. soccer, little league, football, etc.

4. **Beaches**

5. **Hiking/Camping**

6. **Family Get-Togethers** These are usually held in parks or backyards, so the setting is fairly reasonable and realistic.

7. **Parades** These are definitely an exercise for advanced level training with a well-socialized dog.

ADVANCED LEVEL EXERCISES

▪ Hidden or "Blind" Stay ▪

Finally, there's the **Hidden Stay** where the owner actually steps out of sight. This should be the last challenge with the command, once dog and owner

have reached a relatively high level of success with all "3 D's" in a variety of locations. With this exercises, an owner directly challenges a dog's natural instincts to "follow the pack". Many owners notice typical pack behavior throughout the day, as their dogs follow them about, room to room. Often this behavior endears dogs to their owners, although at times most people have admitted it can be a bit annoying (i.e. when they're trying to use the bathroom). From the perspective of the dog, a leader that relocates (even from one room to another) and specifically tells a subordinate *not* to follow, is contrary to basic dog psychology. Packs are supposed to stay together. With many dogs, especially timid ones, this exercise can produce uncertainty and even fear. For that very reason, to help dogs grow, and to develop confidence and trust, this exercise is of profound importance. A side benefit to this exercise is that it does help reduce the intensity of "Separation Anxiety" (discussed in Chapter 7) wherein a dog goes into a sudden (often destructive) panic when they realize they have been left alone.

Photography: Robert Neary

Here's the step-by-step for this exercise:

1. In order to have near complete control over the distractions, conduct the exercise inside the house for the first week or so. Put the 20-foot leash on the dog and put her into a Sit/Stay up against the wall, maybe 3-4 feet back from a corner.

2. Begin feeding out the leash as you back away. Tell the dog calmly but firmly to "Stay" as you retreat slowly. Step around the corner, *just to the point where you lose visual contact with the dog.* **Stop.**

3. Stand still, coaching and reminding the dog from the hiding spot to "Stay". Keep your eyes on the leash for any dramatic movement.

4. Remain out of sight for only 15-20 seconds the first few tries. Do not stay gone so long that the dog becomes apprehensive.

5. If you observe any dramatic movement in the leash, it's most likely a dead giveaway that the dog has broken the Stay. React immediately with a "No!" and step around the corner. Correct the dog with a collar check, get her back into position and start the exercise again.

6. Repeat Item #5 one more time if the dog makes a second mistake. If there is a third mistake, however, go immediately to a stronger correction. Use a Level 2 Scruff Tag or Scruff Shake, relocating the dog back to original spot.

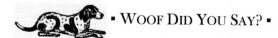

7. When you have achieved the 15-20 seconds, calmly reappear from around the corner, praising the dog *calmly* as well. Do not overdo it on the emotion or energy. The entire exercise is designed *not* to get the dog to overreact at any point. If the dog is sitting in tense expectation of your return (because of the anticipated, exuberant "reward" and affection) she is far more likely to become impatient for your return or to break once she sees you. Therefore, be low-key with your returning praise, but *do* praise.

8. Add time gradually over several days. If 15 seconds is consistently successful, try 30 seconds, then 45 seconds, and so on. The idea is to slowly strengthen the dog's confidence, desensitizing them to brief periods of being alone.

If no progress is being made after more than a week of diligent practice, use the same suggestion as in the Distance Stay—secure the dog with a short leash so she simply cannot follow you. Proceed with all the other guidelines as given, until the dog can successfully return to using a long leash.

Do not combine this exercise with the "Come" command. Do not give the "Recall" command from the blind spot. Turning the exercise into a pseudo Hide-and-Seek game distorts the purpose and invariably makes it impossible to get the dog to Stay for any reasonable length of time. The second you're out of sight, the dog will decide it's time to come looking for you.

As the dog's confidence is being built up, target one minute as the first duration goal. Stick with the guidelines above as you work towards that time, practicing in a variety of locations throughout your house and backyard area — within the dog's "comfort zone". Once the two of you have achieved that first stage, add more challenges with the following:

1. Begin to seriously cut back on the amount of coaching the dog receives when you're out of sight.

2. Relax about standing around the corner. Trust the dog a little more and actually go *do* something. Pick an activity that is brief, only one room away and will allow you to be back in no more than 1½ minutes.

3. Try the exercise in more open, unfamiliar locations — perhaps during a walk through the neighborhood. (Keep the 20-foot leash handy for this.)

A last detail should be noted with Blind Stays. Once the owner has vacated the area and is gone for 2 minutes or more, a dog will often "get comfortable" as she awaits your return. This means that you may come back to find the dog in a Down position, when you left her in a Sitting position. This is not cause for alarm, nor should you correct the dog for it. Success in this instance is claimed if an owner can trust the dog to remain "in that spot" until they return. There is, however, an even more important reason why correcting the dog is technically wrong

in this situation. Corrections *after the fact* are unfair and inappropriate. An owner has no way of knowing exactly *when* the dog moved from a Sit to a Down. Since it is now history and the owner didn't actually witness the event, let this one alone. Praise the dog just the same.

▪ RECALL ▪

Once a dog is responding reliably with the initial Come exercise (20-foot leash from a Sit/Stay) it is time to change the approach and gradually move into more realistic scenarios. In a "true-life" situation, a dog will likely never be sitting and waiting for your command unless you've choreographed it that way. On their own time, dogs will do their "doggy" things, leaving humans on the sidelines. Therefore the most critical and important goal of this command is to get the dog to respond reliably even when he's on his own time.

INTERMEDIATE LEVEL EXERCISES

▪ Round Robin Game ▪

This exercise aims to relax a bit and get away from the rigid approach of the 20-foot leash exercise. It is presented as a fun game, except that the dog is *required* to play along. For most dogs, that seems rarely to be an issue, but nevertheless have your pup dragging a leash just in case. Corrections are not allowed, as they will detract from the "game-like" feel, making the whole thing appear too serious. Leashes are left on *only* to guide and encourage the dog to participate.

This exercise can be helpful with all dogs, whether they're enthusiastic or just ho-hum about the Come command. The purpose is to make the Recall even more fun and enjoyable, never a burden, or something that the dog sees as an annoying interruption. The exercise requires at least two people to participate, in addition to the dog.

Here's the step-by-step for this one:

1. Remove training collars (unnecessary since corrections are not allowed) and attach a leash to the dog's regular collar or a harness (short leash if inside the house, long leash if outside).

2. Clear the designated area of any debris (especially toys) that might distract him from focusing on *you*.

3. Those participating should station themselves in adjacent rooms or locations approximately 15-20 feet apart, within eye contact of one another if possible.

4. Begin with the dog sitting beside the first person in the sequence. Select the order of "calling" the dog, then begin with person No. 2 enthusiastically giving the "Come" command and getting the dog to respond favorably to them.

5. Use as much positive energy and enthusiastic body language as you need to get the desired response out of the dog. Remember this is supposed to be a *game*, so act out the part. If it helps, pretend you're at the World Series or the Super Bowl and your team is ahead.

6. When the dog reaches you, continue the enthusiasm with an equally energetic offering of praise and affection.

7. Proceed to person #3, then #4, and so on, making sure that each person in turn has success getting the dog to respond.

8. After the dog has successfully completed the circuit, find new "stations" for the sake of variety. Run through the entire exercise again.

This exercise is highly recommended for families, as it's important for younger children to get the dog to Come, as much as the adults. As each person in turn calls the dog, the other participants should not assist in any way, possibly confusing the dog or causing a conflict in the dog's mind regarding "allegiance" to a favorite family member. If the dog does make a mistake and goes off course, the designated "caller" needs to go retrieve the dog with the leash, demonstrating control ideally through enthusiasm and a playful re-direct, *not* a correction.

If a particular family member (usually a child) seems to have greater difficulty getting reliable responses from the dog, food *may* be used, but should be kept to a bare minimum. A dog that learns one person is the "food bank" will likely gravitate to that person, thus creating another problem down the road. Using treats randomly and unexpectedly is best, as the dog works harder and is more motivated out of hope and the "possibility" of a greater pay-off. Rewarding with a treat approximately 20% of the time or less is recommended, and never as a visible bribe.

This exercise can be a fun thing to do 3-4 times a week with the dog, a few minutes at a time. However, the longer the game goes on, the greater the likelihood that the energy and intensity will lead to a break-down of control. Therefore, keep the sessions to just a few minutes at a time. The greater goal is, of course, getting the dog to perform a focused Recall. The game-like quality of this exercise can be very helpful, but don't let it get away from you.

ADVANCED LEVEL EXERCISES

▪ Random Reinforcement ▪

This may be the most realistic approach to the Recall, and should be attempted only after several weeks of positive responses from the dog with the other exercises. If a dog isn't keen on the Come command, using this exercise won't necessarily make it better. It is most effective with dogs who are running at better than 50% in their overall reliability, but are still having some minor issues with being distracted.

It is completely different from both of the other Recall exercises in some important ways. The dog will never be in a Sit/Stay prior to giving the command, nor will the owner be presenting it as a game like the Round Robin. It is an ultimate test of the dog's ability and willingness to separate out the will of the leader and the cohesive boundaries of the pack, apart from his/her own individual desires. For reasons of safety, a dog should be expected to respond to "Come", regardless of the time, the location

or the activity she is involved in. That is what this exercise is designed to achieve.

There are a few different approaches to this exercise depending on how an owner chooses to follow-through with a correction, but the basic "set-up" will remain the same. For two of the approaches, leashes need to be left on the dogs to facilitate a timely correction, but it is strongly recommended the owner *not* hold onto the end of it. It becomes far too obvious to the dog and can easily undermine any attempt at realism. In addition, this exercise is deliberately done during the dog's "free-time", when she is enjoying herself, outside of direct control from her owner. This helps add that realistic feel to the exercise that is so critical.

Even though most people claim their dogs rarely ignore the Come command at home, it may still be best to try the exercise the first few times inside the house as opposed to the backyard. Should it be necessary to retrieve the dog, inside the house will likely be easier than a backyard chase.

1. **Leash Approach** Allow the dog to wander about the house on "free-time" with the training collar on, and a short leash attached to the same (*not* recommended you use a choke chain for this). Sufficient time should have elapsed since the close of the last "training session", hopefully ensuring a completely relaxed state-of-mind in the dog. If you are sure the dog is otherwise engaged, and he is *not* paying direct attention to

you, step into view, within 20-30 feet of him. Look directly at the dog, say her name with a friendly and confident tone, then immediately give the "Come" command, with the same level of friendly confidence. Some body language may also be added (extending your arms and/or bending slightly forward) but don't overdo it. Say the command *only once.* Pause 2-3 seconds, giving the dog a brief amount of time to process the event and decide on her response. If, after the elapsed time, it's obvious she has no intention of responding, change the tone of voice and give a direct, firm and commanding No! Hopefully this gets the dog at least to redirect her attention onto you. If so, quickly repeat the "Come", reverting back to a friendly, non-threatening tone of voice. This takes some quick thinking and good acting on the part of the owner to make sure the dog 1) doesn't feel threatened by the either of the command words--just a standard friendly invitation is best and 2) has a full sense of how serious you are when she hears the No!

Now, if you are one of those lucky people whose dog almost never ignores you on this, she's probably trotting happily in your direction, you are breathing a big sigh of relief and (Congratulations!) all that is left is to lavish affection and praise on the dog when she reaches you. On the other hand, if your dog is like so many others out there, she just might still be lying over there, barely glancing in your direction. Take heart! There is a proper response for this level of canine nonchalance.

From this point forward, you must psychologically switch gears. The tone of voice and
body language must change abruptly—the fol-
low-through/correction part of the exercise has
begun. Therefore, ***do not*** repeat "Come" anymore. If your body language is now going to indicate displeasure with the dog's lack of response, connecting that displeasure directly with
the word "Come" can undermine the dog's trust.

Do not waste time by calling the dog a third,
fourth, or fifth time. For the safety of the dog,
limit response time to only 2 tries, and only when
you are still standing with a friendly demeanor.
After all, how far can a dog run in the time it
takes to say the command that many more times?
Therefore, resolve now to "make" the dog Come.

This follow-through, I've found, works extremely well, especially if you have just the right
level of firmness, *without* anger. Begin walking
deliberately toward the dog, repeating "No!" a
few more times on your approach. Do Not run.
Charging at the dog in a dead run will more than
likely create a panic, and then you *will* find yourself having to run after her. If necessary (to deal
with an evasive tactic on the part of the dog) step
on the leash. Then, quickly pick up the end, and
give a good, fast jerk, saying "No!" as you do so.
Immediately let the leash go limp. Switch gears
again, going back to a friendly "Come!" See if
you get the desired response. Repeat steps again
if you need to, continuing to offer inviting body

language in between the corrections. Get the dog to Come *all the way* to where the command was initially given. <u>*Always*</u> offer lavish praise on the dog when she reaches you, *regardless* of any possible corrections it took to get her there. The best results with this approach are when the dog *doesn't see you pick up the leash.* In other words, the correction is not directly linked with *you* and—even more—it seems to come from out of nowhere. This helps the dog grasp the concept of rules being "all-encompassing".

2. **Remote Collar Approach** Essentially the same, with the exception that the owner will not have to pursue the dog at all. From the original spot where the command was given, the "warning" button can be pressed (I still encourage saying No! along with this) if the dog disregards the first invitation to "Come". Repeat the command a second time, then, if needed, proceed to the *lowest* range level on the collar that is needed to get the dog's attention. Dragging a leash may also still be an option.

3. **Scruff Correction Approach** This is my preferred correction for this exercise because it forces the owner to demonstrate their control to the dog *without* relying on outside devices. Because of that, the dog will equate the authority on a much deeper level, not fixating on any extraneous "tools".

   Training collars aren't necessary, although a leash is still highly recommended to facilitate

catching the dog if needed. Proceed with the exact same presentation, offering two friendly tries, and placing a solid, attention-getting No! in between. When and if the dog ignores the second try, go retrieve the dog. However, when the owner catches him, it is essential to grab hold of the dog by the scruff (one hand can be partly under the collar, but there must be some *physical hold* on the dog's pelt as well). Start returning with the dog, hanging on the entire way back. Do Not say "Come" as you are returning--the correction phase is not through yet, so just keep telling him No! at this point. Once you have reached the starting point, lavish praise on the dog, forgiving and forgetting his mistake. Then, walk away and leave the dog alone for a spell! Do not try to "make up" with him.

Reactions by dogs to the Scruff Approach of this exercise vary. I've had some dog students who were instantly "cured" and would rather have died than ignore the "Come" again. Most, however, took more than a few of these corrections to reliably change. Given the firm nature of this exercise, I don't recommend doing it more than 3-4 times on any given day (unless you're having rousing success). After a dog has been corrected once with this exercise, the next time (which shouldn't be for a couple hours or more) he may react with concerned body language. This is very normal. Don't be too worried, but the owner *should remember* to appear sufficiently enthusiastic and inviting. Don't get any more stern with the "No!" or the correction you chose.

On the other hand, if the second try produces what appears to be a state of panic, it's a clear indication that the correction used was excessive for that particular dog. In that case, ease up on the negative energy, squat down and appear as open and non-dominant as possible. After all, we have to assume that the dog truly wants to get this right. No dog really wants to get corrected repeatedly if he can figure out how to avoid it.

If an owner is doing this exercise properly, this will not confuse the dog or make him afraid to Come. The most important aspects are to 1) separate the friendly command word from the corrective phase of the exercise, and 2) use only enough force to get the dog to change his mind and start responding. Item 2 is very subjective, requiring an owner to intimately know what amount of force is needed for their own dog. It may be that just a stern No! is sufficient. Or, it might require some firm scruffing. The point is to learn to "read" the dog's response, so you know when you have connected and made your point.

Important to point out as well, that the correction of choice should produce some signals that indicate submission—shifted ears, dropped tail and/or head area. Severe reactions such as squealing, trying to bite or throwing himself on the ground, indicate the dog is bordering on fear. This is *not* the purpose of the exercise (suggestion to reread Chapter 3 on body language). Overdoing or under doing the correction won't produce good results. The dog will either learn to ignore you, or become intimidated. Know

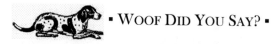

what works for your dog and practice your controlled response.

Be aware of the variable nature of selecting which correction to use in any given situation. For instance, at home, just a firm voice may be sufficient. However, when the dog is playing in his backyard or at a park , a more assertive correction may be required to get him to respond.

There are some "gray areas" with this exercise, when an owner should be willing to back off. Sometimes all that is needed is to "call the dog's bluff". Plenty of times, an owner will go through the first three steps of the exercise: command--warn--repeat command, all the while watching the dog ignore them. Then, when the owner decides to take that first step in the dog's direction (except when using a remote collar) he suddenly changes his mind and comes running over. He's watching your every move, knowing full-well just how long he's got before his time "runs out". There isn't necessarily a problem with this, unless it becomes obvious that the dog is too familiar with the process, deliberately holding out until the last possible moment. Still, I tend to give the dog the benefit of the doubt if the danger factor is low, and I don't actually have to march over and grab him.

Lastly, make this exercise a *brief* interruption in the dog's "free time", and you will see more positive results and a greater willingness to respond. What this means is that, once you have gotten the dog over

to you (by whatever means necessary) lavish the praise and then release the dog to go back to his play-time. If you do this repeatedly, the dog views the exercise as less burdensome. To some personality types, the Recall may be a slight nuisance, but if they know that they will be allowed to return to their "game" in just a moment, then it becomes less arduous. Don't force the dog to linger with you any longer than necessary to demonstrate his proficiency.

As a dog becomes more and more reliable with this exercise, present it in ever more challenging locations. As long as there's little likelihood of it getting caught on something, owners can consider leaving 20 foot leashes on the dogs in some areas. This is probably the most common mistake that owners make when practicing "Come". They assume too quickly that their dog will respond to the command with equal reliability, regardless of where they are. Hence, they unhook the leashes prematurely, leaving themselves no "safety net". If the point is to create, in the dog's mind, the idea of a command being unalterable, then allowing too much room for error can severely undermine this. From a training perspective, it is one of the most difficult situations to combat when an owner allows a dog to get loose. Each time it happens, the dog becomes more aware of the subjective nature of the command. With time, it can become nearly impossible to get good results without leashes or collars. Thus, being able to catch your dog is always an issue. Leaving a "safety net" on the dog until you're sure of his response is not an admission of failure. It's just good common sense.

• Down •

Intermediate Level Exercises

• Weaning off Treats •

The first step to any advanced work with this command is the complete elimination of treats. In Chapter 5, guidelines were to work steadily with food rewards for 3-4 days, assuming practice is done 2-3 times a day, 12-15 repetitions in a session (one "Down/Up" push-up counts as one sequence). At the low end, that's 72 repetitions. At the high end, it's 180. The average dog will likely need 100 or more repetitions before one can safely assume he's grasped the meaning. If you are way below these figures, keep working at it. Get to a point where it appears the dog is more than willing to drop into the Down for you. There should be a relatively high level of cooperation (doesn't have to be perfect) with the dog sliding quickly into position as the hand motion is executed. If this best describes your situation, and the figures listed above seem about right, begin the weaning off process.

With the dog on a "Sit/Stay", hold two treats in your hand . Reward as usual for the first sequence. Proceed with the next sequence *empty handed*. For the third sequence, use treats. For the fourth, do not, and so on. This "every other time" pattern can be continued for one or two days. If all seems well, cut back to a reward only every *third* sequence, then every *fourth* sequence, and so on, over the course of the next several days. Through this entire weaning

off process, continue to practice equally inside and outside as before. With the exception of the treats being less frequent, nothing should appear different to the dog.

Another approach to weaning off allows for treats on the first sequence as usual. Immediately refill your hand, but now use the treat as a "lure", coaxing the dog through two, three or even four sequences with the same treat before finally releasing it to her.

With either approach, it often helps to select a moister, more pungent or flavorful food reward to heighten the dog's desire to "work hard" for that bonus. Dry biscuits are often the least effective at this stage. Soft chew treats, bacon bits, small pieces of cooked chicken, or lunchmeats are more appealing alternatives.

▪ Resistance to Weaning Off ▪

At some point in the weaning off process, the vast majority of owners encounter resistance. After all, from the dog's perspective, the rules have suddenly changed without consulting him. Occasionally there are dogs who don't seem to mind at all that food has been removed, performing just as reliably with or without. However, depending on the dog's personality, resistance may begin very rapidly, perhaps when the pattern is only at one treat for every third sequence. When and if resistance happens, it's critical that the owner not give in to the dog's wishes and grab a treat--*especially* if you are sure this isn't an issue of confusion. This may seem like the easy thing to do, but, taken from a slightly different perspective, with that simple action, the *owner* becomes the *trainee*, and the *dog* becomes the *trainer*. If you have a solid sense that the dog understands this command when treats were used, then rest assured that he still understands it when treats are *not* used. The resistance is simply a demonstration of his displeasure with the change. *It doesn't mean he's confused!*

When and if you encounter resistance, remain calm and in control. Do not get exasperated with the dog, and do not let your voice give away any frustration. Hold firmly to the decision *not* to grab a treat. Use the hand signal as usual, keeping the voice steady, even and direct. Often a flat, monotone voice helps with this, as opposed to allowing the voice to rise slightly at the end, as it does in normal conversation. Purposefully controlling inflection in the voice takes practice, but can be of great help getting a dog to be calm and focused.

Go through the pattern twice with the dog. Give the command once, then pause 2-3 seconds to allow time for his response. If he isn't going into position, give a firm (no shouting) "No!" Then repeat the command again, using the calm but direct tone. If there is still no cooperation, one of the following responses can be tried:

1. Give a firm *downward* pop on the training collar with a No! Relax the collar, try the command word one more time. If the dog is still not coop-

erating, repeat the collar correction, but this time use steady, *uninterrupted* tension until the dog is solidly in position. Make sure *only* the word No is being said while you are pulling on the collar. **Caution:** *Do not* use this correction if you are using a choke collar.

2. Apply tension on the training collar, and at the same time place a hand behind the dog's front knees. Simultaneously pull on collar, and firmly/quickly bump right behind the dog's knee with your hand. The combination of actions will cause the dog to begin sliding in a downward direction. Say No! as you do this.

3. Manipulate the dog quickly into position using a Level 2 Scruff Down (Chapter 4).

4. The correction should be done quickly and efficiently, using leverage primarily to get the dog slightly off balance, successfully getting her into position. With one hand on the dog's scruff area, pull quickly to one side, angling towards the ground as well.

The element of surprise helps immensely with this. If the dog isn't expecting this from you, it will be much easier to maneuver. Sometimes, with tall, long-legged dogs, it may require getting the other hand behind a front leg, aiding in the leverage issue. The most important thing with this particular correction is *not* to get into a wrestling match with the dog, yanking ineffectively back and forth. Technique is critical—the dog should be down within a second or two.

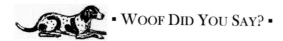

If, in the process of any of these three corrections, the dog stands up, get her quickly back into the Sit, and try again. Use whichever of the three follow-throughs seems to work best for your particular dog, remembering to use the least amount of force necessary to accomplish the task. With any and all of the above follow-throughs, make sure immediate and sincere praise is offered as soon as the dog is in position.

Having to deal with resistance is not pleasant, but allowing a dog to simply refuse the owner this bit of submissive body language is not considered acceptable. Some time ago, a student told me she decided the "Down" command wasn't worth the effort to her (hence not important anymore) simply because her dog flat out refused to cooperate. She was worn out "arguing" with the dog. I encouraged her to look at it from the dog's perspective, asking her why she thought the dog was so adamant about *not* doing it? When the answer came back that "It must be a big deal to the dog", the point was made. In other words, if the dog sees this as a major issue, so should the owner. And, therefore, don't give up.

Continue to practice every day with the dog, going through 8-10 sequences in a row, at least twice a day. This is not necessarily an easy command to teach a dog. Stubborn, headstrong personality types are far more likely to resist this command than the calm, relaxed ones.

If you encounter extreme, prolonged resistance and/or defiant aggression, consider seeking some

outside training assistance. As always, a lot of aggression can stem from mixed signals and confusion with the passive messages sent by the owner. As with all of the commands, an owner can expect better results and better responsiveness all around if they have carefully learned the fine points of "passive messaging" throughout the day and in general in the relationship with their dog.

INTERMEDIATE TO ADVANCED LEVEL EXERCISES

• Down/Stay •

The focus here is to prolong the duration, selecting locations where it is a mental challenge for the dog to remain attentive and obedient. Go about this gradually, progressively increasing the length of time and distraction level over days and weeks. It is always recommended to have a leash on the dog for each new challenge, allowing for quick and efficient corrections as needed. Some of my favorite places to practice are playgrounds, street corners, school bus stops, in front of retail shops, or any place that might draw a large group of people. Another challenge is to practice Down/Stay when another dog is passing by. Discourage any kind of sniffing greeting at this time.

Occasionally use one of the dog's toys as a distraction during this exercise. Consider balls, chew toys or a favorite squeaky. This last suggestion is not unfair teasing. What it demonstrates is the "rule of rank" and your ability to "control the resources". The leader (that's you) retains the prerogative to select an item (whatever that might be) for personal entertainment at any time. The toy, thus, becomes a valued "resource". The first time an owner tries this challenge, the dog will likely confuse it with an invitation to play. However, with steady practice and reinforcement, the message will come through.

▪ Side Down ▪

This exercise gets its name because when the command is given, dog and owner are standing *side by side*, instead of facing each other. It is an increased challenge for the dog primarily for two reasons:

1. Changing something as basic as the way the exercise "appears" to the dog can temporarily cause confusion and possibly resistance. Therefore, it is always important to keep a command new and dynamic, hopefully ensuring that the dog (and owner) doesn't get "stuck in a rut", unable to be flexible.

2. Side Down's are typically done during a Heeling exercise, so the dog will not be in her "comfort zone". Owner and dog may be several blocks from the house, at an intersection, near a playground, or standing and chatting with a neighbor. This aspect of the exercise challenges the dog in a dramatic way to *trust* the owner's (leader's) decisions. Remember that "Down" is a position of submission and, hence, *vulnerability*. It's quite common for a dog to resist going into position if she feels the location is unsafe. Thus, a dog that *easily* drops into position, regardless of

the location, is very well socialized *and* has complete faith in the leader's direction.

On a typical Heeling exercise, remember to periodically reinforce the Auto-Sit. To add the Side Down, on every fifth Stop/Sit sequence, reach across the front of your body with the right hand. Give the hand signal and the verbal command simultaneously, directing the dog into the "Down", at the left heel position. Make your voice calm and firm. Be patient. Give the dog 2-3 seconds for initial response time. If you encounter resistance, give a warning "No!", repeat the command again in the same fashion.

Follow-throughs can be any of the techniques given above in the "weaning off" section. I have also found that a sporadic treat thrown in to take the dog's mind off the location can be helpful the *first few times* you try this. **However,** it should not become a regular or predictable event. Reverting back to reliance on treats will all too easily undermine the overall progress you have made. "No treat? No Down!" might be the response from the dog.

Once the dog is in the Down position, follow-up with a "Stay" for a period of time. Recommended to keep the dog on a "Down/Stay" for at least 30 seconds (if she cooperated and slid willingly into position) or at least 1 minute if she resisted and a follow-through was needed. The reason for this is to get the dog to settle *mentally* into the awareness of "being Down". Stubborn, headstrong personalities benefit greatly from being held in a "Down/Stay" for awhile with this exercise. An owner who allows the dog to pop right back up like a yo-yo never really insists that the dog trust and have faith in the leader's decision. If a leader decides a location is safe, the dog should accept it.

That being said, use good judgment selecting locations for practice sessions. Avoid areas like dog parks, where there are too many uncontrolled variables. If your dog is displaying a vulnerable/passive position to others, she may appear as an easy target to some less sociable animals. It's best not to put your dog in that situation if there are too many unknowns.

▪ Distance Down ▪

Last of the 3 D's in this category, the goal here is to *give the command from a distance,* successfully getting the dog to drop on the spot. This should be seen partly as an issue of convenience (not having to be within arm's length of the dog to get a response) but also for safety reasons. I encourage my students to set a goal of 40+ feet—the distance across most residential roadways.

This variation of the command sometimes brings with it some unwanted quirks--specifically the tendency for the dog to try to move forward, toward the owner. For safety reasons, it should not be allowed . Not all dogs will attempt the forward scoot, but most will give it a shot at least in the beginning. The reasons are:

1. If the dog is still hoping for a food reward, he knows he can't reach it from 3 or more feet away. Therefore, it's mandatory that treat incentives be a thing of the past before trying this.

2. Moving slyly into your "personal space" allows the dog an opportunity to turn on the charm, dramatize fawning or submissive behavior in other ways, and hopefully "talk you out of it". This can be observed in many cases with the dog dropping the head and shoulders, turning the body slightly and moving in in a wiggling, puppy-like manner. It may be cute, but is certainly not the behavior that was requested.

3. Even in the event that the dog is actually intending to do what you have said, there is also some likelihood that he may attempt a forward scoot. This is due to the "positioning" that dogs do when displaying this level of submissive gesturing. If one dog is going to submit for a higher ranking individual, the "Down" behavior is done right in front of the authority figure, not from several feet away. In a training setting, then, the dog *might* be maneuvering into position before doing the owner's bidding. Again, however, for safety reasons, it should not be allowed.

Be on the lookout for these displays, and learn to react quickly but appropriately. Be firm, but not overbearing. Make the dog understand that he can execute the Down without the "lead-in" of the forward scoot.

Here's a step-by-step for achieving the Distance Down:

1. Have the dog's short leash on, and give him a Sit/Stay command. Step back one stride's length. Stand fully upright with a relaxed but "in control" demeanor.

2. Hold the leash in the left hand, relaxed but not sloppy. Look directly at the dog and give hand signal with right hand, simultaneously with verbal command. Avoid saying the dog's name for this exercise (it seems to encourage more scooting behavior) even if he's not looking at you. Use a calm but firm and direct voice. Do not shout or have any tension in your voice.

3. Down-play your gestures and body language with the hand signal. Bend just slightly at the waist, lowering the hand/arm just until it is even with your thigh or knee. Bending too far forward or squatting too closely resembles an invitation to play, encouraging unwanted antics from the dog. Keep your head and shoulders in a dominant posture while doing this.

4. Continue to look directly at the dog at this point and wait 2-3 seconds for evidence of a response.

5. Be alert to any attempt by the dog to scoot forward. This *must not* be allowed. If you notice this, your reaction must be swift and firm. Step directly at the dog with a firm and quick No!. Grab the leash at the collar, returning the dog to the original spot as quickly as possible. Repeat the "Stay". Try again from Item #2.

6. Follow this procedure one more time. If the dog is still resisting, with or without a forward scoot, step quickly toward the dog and use one of the three follow-throughs that were given in the section on "Weaning Off". *Make sure* at this point that you are only saying No! as you get the dog into position.

7. Once he is Down, pause briefly and judge whether he has relaxed into position. You do not want him to pop up the second you let go. Praise him for a "Good Down", then give the Stay command. Slowly and cautiously stand up.

8. Keep him in a Down/Stay for 30 seconds or more. Bring the dog "Up". Pause 10-15 seconds, then try the process again.

9. Be prepared to do about 8 sequences in a row, at least twice a day. Keep the follow-throughs consistently firm and predictable. Steady persistence nearly always wins on this.

Once the initial 3-4 feet has been solidly achieved, with a successful response rate of nearly 90%, the owner can increasing the distance farther. Plan to step back another stride's length (15-18 inches) every few days, following the exact same approach. The ever-increasing distance should be subtle, hoping that the dog will barely notice on any given day. Before long, you will have increased the distance to where a short leash becomes restrictive. At this point, the owner can either tie the short leash to secure objects to safely continue backing up, or else switch to a 20-foot leash.

How quickly a dog grasps the distance exercise is variable and largely based on persistence and personality-type. Relaxed, laid-back dogs seem to respond quicker. Dogs with stubborn, highly energetic or assertive personalities are likely to resist longer. Some students have responded within a few days, others struggled for 3-4 weeks before progress was visible. If it is important to you, keep practicing. Slow and steady with consistent reinforcing almost always wins in the long run.

CHAPTER 7

PROBLEM BEHAVIOR

▪ SPECIAL HELPS ▪

Photo courtesy Bennett & Hastings

Throughout this book the focus has tried to be on looking through the dog's perspective whenever possible. Making sure that the dog's needs are met (physical and psychological) helps to ensure a

higher level of success. Knowing how to "read" your own dog as you train and interact with him will encourage a deeper understanding and appreciation. It will also keep the owner alert to the need for any modification of a technique that will better suit your own dog and a specific situation. No two dogs are exactly alike. Flexibility and sensitivity are crucial elements in training. Taking the advice from someone who doesn't "know" your dog, or applying techniques that worked on a dog from years past may not be effective. Throughout this book suggestions have been given, whenever possible, to help in those cases where the "standard" approach doesn't seem to work. All attempt to stay true to form, suggesting solutions that are reasonable and humane, and yet do not compromise the "canine" learning process.

Being consistent with the passive messages during daily interaction can and should be seen as an equally important part of the training process. Learn to synthesize all elements of communication and interaction with the dog in everyday activities. Thinking of training as something that is done "outside" of the regular routine can be counterproductive. It goes against the philosophy of "always a leader". Just because an owner isn't holding a leash or giving a direct "command", doesn't mean the dog has stopped watching for signals.

This chapter, then, is meant to tie loose ends with the "rest" of the signals, and give assistance for behaviors that don't fit exactly into the category of "command training". It will help with issues of annoying, destructive or dangerous behavior that owners often experience. Suggestions will be designed to fit with a specific dog's personality type, customizing solutions to a variety of dogs and situations.

■ "OTHER" EXERCISES—PROTOCOL WORK ■

In addition to the constructive mental exercises outlined in Chapters 5 and 6, there are a few other activities or "daily rituals" I encourage students to do with their dogs that can also enhance and reinforce the owner's higher rank and position of authority. These exercises will teach the dog to handle minor frustrations in life, learn patience and the idea that "good things come to those who wait". With the following exercises, an owner can demonstrate the issue of "protocol" and/or controlling of resources—even those that are not so tangible. A *resource*, in broad terms, is simply *something that the dog sees as valuable at a particular moment in time*. With some of these activities, the owner also will be simulating actual pack behavior and/or demonstrating the power of passive messaging in a simple, common sense approach.

■ Quick Checks ■

These are presented as a basic "examination" of the dog. They can be done a few times a week or every day. The practical reasons for doing this are:

1. Basic grooming of the dog will become less arduous. Basic grooming refers to brushing, teeth and ear cleaning, and trimming of nails.

2. Veterinarians will definitely appreciate a cooperative patient who allows for mouth and ear

 WOOF DID YOU SAY?

examination without antics—aggressive or otherwise. No one likes getting bitten, vets included.

3. Asserts owner's status, specifically regarding *Personal Space*.

A "Quick Check" involves manipulation of the dog's paws and ears and opening the dog's mouth. In a very direct way, insisting the dog allow, even tolerate this, from his owner, mimics behavior observed when two dogs of very different rank meet on neutral ground. Body posturing and "who is sniffing who" are clear indicators of which dog is the more dominant animal. The higher ranking dog will stand rigidly, moving in a stiffly cautious but authoritative manner. The subordinate dog will stand passively, ears back, eyes averted and tail generally in a downward position. It is definitely not a mutual investigation. It is a very common and observable behavior demonstrating natural order between dogs.

When an owner performs a "Quick Check", they must insist on playing the role of the leader or more dominant animal. Therefore, the dog must *not* be allowed to sniff, lick, mouth or in any way fuss or fight with the owner. There is absolutely no pain or discomfort involved in the performance of a quick check. If a dog resists the activity, it is for psychological, *not* physical reasons. If you have a puppy, the sooner the better to begin getting him accustomed to having this done frequently.

Another aspect to the "Quick Check" that is important to point out, is that you will be inside the

213

dog's "personal space" to do it. This part of communication was discussed in Chapter 3. The critical part here is that the dog, ideally ranking *below* the owner in pack structure, is not given the prerogative to keep you out of his space. Remember that as you do this. Be respectful while you perform this activity, but just as important, insist that the dog allow it!

To effectively perform a "Quick Check", have collar and leash on the dog. Place him into a Sit/Stay, holding the leash about 6" away from the clasp (collar should be relaxed). Tell the dog calmly but firmly to "Stay". With the other hand, pick up one of the front paws. Hold it in your hand, reminding the dog to "Stay". If he attempts to sniff, lick or mouth you, give a quick and firm jerk on the collar, saying "No!" *Do not let go of the paw!* Continue to follow these steps until the dog sits passively and allows you to hold up each paw for 5-10 seconds apiece with no fussing.

Many dogs resist the paw check. For some, it may be due to ticklishness. For others, resistance can either be an indication of an assertive attitude, or a learned aversion because of an unpleasant experience. For Brittany, the English Bull Dog, the resistance was two-fold:

1. She was simply stubborn to begin with and

2. She had had her nails trimmed too short a number of times, cutting into the quick. She had developed a very real fear reaction when people picked up her paws, relating it to an unpleasant and painful nail trim.

In these situations, re-conditioning the dog to see paw-handling as neutral, pleasant and non-threatening is part of the key. Do not become aggressive with the dog, but don't let go of the paw. Perhaps offer a small treat if she allows the paw to be held for 3-5 seconds without a fight. Calmly encourage the dog to sit quietly, but do not offer soothing "baby talk". This often makes the situation worse.

The ear check is much the same. Follow the same procedure with the dog on a Sit/Stay and one hand on the leash. Manipulate the ears gently, folding back floppy ones. Look briefly inside to check for dirt and/or dirt accumulation that may require cleaning. Very few dogs seem to have difficulty with this portion of the Quick Check. I suspect it may even feel good to many dogs.

Last in the list of Quick Check items is opening the dog's mouth. The dog should be on a Sit/Stay for this as well, with the leash on. Start with the hand at the end of the dog's nose. Slide your fingers back along the gum line, lifting up the jowls. As you pass the large upper canine teeth, press your thumb and index finger in behind them. This makes the dog release the jaws. The thumb of the other hand is then placed over the front teeth of the *lower jaw*. Say, "Open" and hold, regardless of the thrashing that may occur! Count to 3. Slowly close the mouth, rub the top of the dog's nose and offer praise. If your dog has an enormous nose or a blunt nose, modify as best you can to work the mouth open with a minimum of threat.

Like the paw check, (and probably for the same reasons) this often produces some resistance and thrashing. Be calm, but, above all, *be persistent*. The natural reaction for most people if a dog starts pulling side-to-side with his head/nose is to quickly let go. This is *not* recommended. When hands get snatched away quickly from the dog's mouth (especially when he's not enjoying the contact) it can all too easily trigger the "snap" or "bite" reflex. For this very reason, *it is not recommended that children do the mouth check.*

▪ Feeding Ritual ▪

Another activity that can help in establishing rank deals with territory and order of "who eats first". When a pack eats, the hierarchy is observed by which dogs eat first. Higher ranking dogs often "claim" the carcass first, establishing possession and rank "territory" over the food supply. All other members will typically stay back and allow the leaders to feed on the choicest portions. Those who attempt to sneak in are usually chased off. Alphas are not generally given a time limit on their meal, either.

When the leaders have eaten their fill, they will "release" the remains of the carcass to the rest of the pack by walking away. This is the signal for all subordinates to jump in and grab a portion before it's all gone. This stage of the pack feeding is often fraught with contention, as "beta's" squabble over the meal.

Owners can simulate this pack ritual with a simple exercise each time the dog's food is offered. The

"resource" being controlled here is the dog's food portion. First, assert that the food is *your portion*. Place the dog into a Sit/Stay (leash on if necessary). Slowly lower the food dish to the floor, continuing to keep the dog in a Sit/Stay. If you can successfully place the dish on the floor without the dog getting up, slowly count to 5. All the while, the dog must remain in his Sit/Stay. It should be a full, uninterrupted 5 seconds. While the dog is waiting, he is acknowledging your "claim" over the food as the leader. At the end, release the dog with an enthusiastic, "Go Eat!", and simply walk away.

The second part of the exercise is to rigidly limit the length of time the dog has to eat his meal. You can decide how long you feel is reasonable, as long as it doesn't go over 30 minutes. Do not leave food lying around all day for the dog to nibble on. Remember that only the leaders need not worry about time limits on their meals. The only exception to this is for dogs who, for a medical reason, are on prescription diets.

Depending on the dog and how relaxed an owner has been with meals, the initial waiting part of the exercise may seem to miss its mark. Dogs who have been accustomed to food lying around all day will not initially see the significance of the "wait". They typically walk away from the bowl after being released, intending to come back over the course of a few hours to eat. Making sure the food is picked up in no more than 30 minutes will have the bigger impact on these "nibblers". They will quickly become tuned in to the exercise after one or two missed meals, learning there is a time limit now imposed.

▪ Doorway Etiquette ▪

This little exercise involves teaching dogs self-control at doors leading out of the house. Self-control is taught in two separate situations:

1. during greeting-type encounters when someone might be at your front door, and

2. when the dog herself is passing in and/or out through an open doorway.

Owners find these exercises very helpful controlling a typically chaotic and otherwise frustrating daily activity. The "resource" being controlled here is the dog's access to outside. For three reasons, these next exercises are quite practical:

1. For safety reasons, dogs should be taught *not* to dart in or out of open doorways. Rushing out a front door is obviously potentially life threatening for a dog, especially if the house is situated on a busy street. But darting *in* through doorways is also potentially dangerous for humans who might be standing nearby—especially small children. The size of the dog has little bearing. Small dogs can dart between legs and trip a person just as easily as a large dog can bump and knock someone over.

2. For cleanliness, and just good citizen behavior, a dog that is conditioned to only take a couple

steps into the house and then pause or sit, can easily be toweled off or have her paws wiped, should she be wet or muddy.

3. For minor reasons of protocol, a dog should be taught to be the last one through a doorway whenever feasible. Humans and/or leaders should precede the dog across a doorway, going in or out.

Teaching good manners during a greeting type situation requires control of both the dog *and* the human factor. As mentioned earlier, it is unreasonable to demand self-control from a dog (much less a puppy) if the messages coming from the humans encourage the opposite. In practical terms, how can an owner expect a puppy to sit calmly at the door when the person on the other side is staring straight at them, cooing away in baby talk? An owner should do their best to discourage other people from reinforcing out-of-control behavior from the dog. This can begin by explaining that petting and praise is given when the dog is able to maintain the Sit/Stay—some wiggling notwithstanding—*not before.*

When approaching the door, place the dog into a Sit/Stay (training collar and leash should be on) *before* the door even opens. Keep the leash relaxed *until and unless* the dog requires a correction. *Do not* stand at the door, holding the dog back with throat strangling restraint. This teaches nothing. Coach and remind the dog to "Stay", as you also direct the other person to control their response to the dog. This exercise can be practiced a few times in a row, if you can get a neighbor or friend to knock on the door three or four times within a few minutes. The dog will learn quickly that very few people will offer the contact and interaction he's looking for until he exhibits self-control.

The second exercise with doorway etiquette is teaching the dog controlled entrances and exits. Here's a practical step-by-step:

1. Put collar and leash on the dog. Walk to the door with the dog and tell him to "Sit/Stay". Door should be closed at this point.

2. Remind the dog to "Stay" as you reach out and open the door. Correct the dog as needed if curiosity or anticipation causes him to get out of position. Put him back into a "Stay" and go back to opening the door. Repeat as needed until he gets the idea.

3. With the door open, tell the dog again to "Stay", and step across the doorway yourself, leaving the dog *inside*. Continue to hold the leash, but avoid pulling on the collar. It will easily confuse him about what your wishes are. Correct again, as needed, if he starts to head out with you.

4. Pause outside, making the dog wait a few seconds before the command "Out" is given. Some slight collar pressure can be used if the dog doesn't readily respond on his own. *Do Not* tolerate the dog jumping the gun.

5. As soon as he's passed over the threshold, give another "Sit" command, getting him into position quickly; within 3-4 feet of the doorway.

6. Reverse the exercise when coming back "In".

This exercise is best done repetitively. I suggest doing this 6-8 times in a row, sporadically through-out the day, at whichever door seems best, as long as it leads out of the house. Backyard gates are also rec-ommended. Don't limit practice to the few times a day when the dog needs to be let out for bathroom runs or a walk. He will need many more "dry runs" before it becomes an ingrained behavior.

• PROBLEM BEHAVIOR •

Most behaviors that owners view as "problems" are not necessarily seen as such by the dog. They are, in truth, probably quite normal and useful activities in a natural state. Depending on the setting, some "problem" behaviors can be seen as definite benefits. For instance, most owners dislike "diggers"—unless your dog is being trained to hunt truffles. Nipping is discouraged—unless your dog herds sheep. Aggres-sive displays are bad—unless it's directed at a bur-glar. What is really more to the point is that owners wish to teach their dogs discriminating skills, rather than to completely eliminate a behavior.

Beyond that, as mentioned in Chapter 1, problem behaviors can be manifestations of "needs" in the dog that are not being met, whether physical or psycho-logical. For example, sometimes, a dog that digs con-stantly is simply bored or under exercised. Other times behaviors are clear indicators that the social structure is *backward*—dog as leader, human as follower. Dogs that behave in an aggressive or otherwise "possessive" fashion with their owners are sometimes just display-ing classic symptoms of a reversed social structure.

The dog has learned, through specific behavior patterns, to successfully manipulate his environment.

And, as usual, there is the distinctly "human" part to problem behaviors. Many owners, because of the way they respond to the dog, unwittingly reinforce or condition them to do the very things that are disliked. After all, how can one resist that cute little face and wagging tail when she greets you after work? Even if she is jumping all over you?? How can you say No! to her when she drops that spitty ball in your lap for the 15th time and barks in your face--even if you've got a 5:00 PM deadline on this merger proposal??

Simple training that involves teaching "deferred gratification" to the dog, as well as offering *plenty* of good, old-fashioned exercise, often causes many problem behaviors to disappear on their own. With this in mind, I will usually defer addressing specific behaviors at the onset, preferring to wait and see what remains *after* correcting a dysfunctional social structure and meeting the dog's physical needs.

A family that owned a 9-month old Maltipoo called me, concerned with displays of dangerous and territorial behavior from their dog. One behavior that particularly concerned them was chasing cars—after all, at 10-pounds, the dog hardly stood a chance! After assessing the situation and relationship between the owners and the dog, it turned out to be a simple case of role reversal—the dog had successfully manipulated her way to the top of the social structure,

with the owners playing the role of fawning servants. Once the owners were taught how to get back in charge, placing the dog in the role of "follower", and giving her plenty of constructive exercise, the car chasing went away on its own.

A 130-pound female Rottweiler was charging the fence line aggressively when people walked by. At times she would even pop boards off, so fierce were her attacks. The whole neighborhood was terrified, and rightfully so. A classic Catch-22 scenario, the dog desperately needed constructive exercise, but wasn't getting it because of the aggressive behavior—which was a manifestation of no exercise! With a program that taught the owners how to "lead", they successfully eliminated the dog's fence charging within a few weeks. They were then able to walk her peacefully (and proudly) around their neighborhood. In the end, everyone got what they needed.

A young couple with a 1 year-old St. Bernard was greatly concerned about aggressive and possessive behavior regarding the wife. The dog became aggressive with the husband when he attempted to show affection to his wife. They were concerned not just for themselves, but also for their baby, which was due in just 6 weeks. During the consultation, it became evident that the dog was extremely spoiled and pampered, receiving near constant petting and affection, being allowed onto any and all items of furniture at will, was served pot roast and grilled salmon, and invited to sleep in the bed with the couple. Again, the solution wasn't any serious re-training of the dog, so much as it involved re-educating the owners about the perils of passive messaging. In just two weeks of a strict "no pampering" ordinance, this gentle giant became just that.

A couple with a young Shiba Inu called about training after they came home to find their energetic and determined pup had clawed an enormous hole through the dry wall of the kitchen. After just a couple weeks with educating both dog and owner, the puppy showed no inclination of returning to her old pastime. We never had to actually correct the dog for her attempts at "redecorating".

These actual cases demonstrate how important exercise, proper passive messaging and discipline are to controlling a dog. None of the above cases really involved having to "correct" the dog to any great degree for the unacceptable behavior. More accurately, they involved giving the dog a new perspective as well as a constructive physical release.

All these cases aside, as owners learn to "revamp" their old relationships with their dogs, some constructive approaches to certain behaviors may still be beneficial. Some of the most common concerns will be listed, followed by at least two or three suggested solutions for each—least forceful method first, increasing in assertiveness. Always remember to:

1. Know your own dog's individual personality and choose the best suggestion to fit with their temperament. What works with one dog may not work so well with another.

2. Always choose the solution that involves the least amount of force *first*. Don't go overboard if it isn't necessary. It's too easy to create other, trickle down problems as a result.

3. Be open to trying more than one suggestion, depending on the situation. For instance, what works to stop jumping in the living room may not work at the park with a playground full of children.

▪ Jumping Up ▪

Typically seen during greeting, or otherwise when the dog is extremely excited and like energy is mirrored back by the human. Sometimes it can also be observed as a reaction to stress or anxiety—dog is looking for protection/security from the human.

1. If the dog is 25 pounds or less, and the behavior is seen primarily during a moment of greeting, it may help for the owner to squat down to the dog's level. Since greeting generally involves face nuzzling and jowl licking, it may make it easier for the dog to say hello if you are in this position. This does *not* imply that you should at this point encourage or allow the dog to jump all over you. There is still a reasonable amount of self-control that should be enforced. If, on the other hand, the dog is a *larger* breed, or you cannot control the exuberance, I *do not* recommend squatting. You might find yourself on your rear end before you know it.

2. Regardless of whether behavior is due to stress or sheer exuberance, try passive/aggressive attempts

to defuse. Offer NO acknowledgement of dog, including eye contact. Keep hands and limbs folded, away from dog. Hold your body fully upright in a calm but confident and aloof manner. If necessary, brush past the dog, abruptly rebuffing attempts to jump into your personal space. Continue to ignore the emotional display until the dog calms down on his own. Length of time that this takes may vary--usually just a few short minutes. It depends on the dog and the degree to which the behavior was reinforced. Generally speaking, the longer the behavior has been in place, with the dog seeing it as a viable means to an end, the longer it may take to change.

3. Perform a quick side/step or body block (turning abruptly sideways or against the dog) with a firm "No!" Follow defusing directions in Suggestion 2.

4. Use a vinegar and water squirt (Chapter 2, Crate Introduction) to create a respectful "safe" zone. Also reinforce with above passive/aggressive approach.

5. Have collar and leash on the dog and use a quick collar correction, along with a "No!" in conjunction with Suggestion 2.

6. Use a firm and decisive Level 2 Scruff Tag (Chapter 4) followed by suggestion 2.

7. Use a firm and decisive Level 2 Scruff Hold (Chapter 4) actually following through by abruptly pushing the dog down to the floor. Follow with Suggestion 2.

8. For breeds over 40 or 45 pounds, an abrupt knee to the chest might also work, saying a firm "No!" as the technique is performed. Follow with Suggestion 2.

Be aware that the more physically exuberant the dog, often the less affective a *physical* correction is on the part of the owner. The dog may very well be looking to initiate a good game of rough and tumble, so be wise to a secondary motive in the dog. Once the initial emotional outburst from the dog seems to be getting under control, add an extra bit of discipline to the encounter, teaching the dog to "Sit" before you will pet him. (See "Other Exercises" — Doorway/Greeting Etiquette in this chapter.)

Remedies 5-7 are not recommended if the behavior is generated by fear. If the dog is feeling insecure, strong physical corrections can add to his insecurity. Limit your reaction to simply ignoring it or possibly a collar correction. Then try to channel the emotion away into other mental disciplines, such as a Sit/Stay.

• Jumping on Furniture•

This issue is also discussed in Chapter 3 (Personal Space) so owners should, in general, discourage "uninvited" coziness at the whim of the dog. However, when left alone in the house dogs often help themselves to sofas and beds. If that is the case, here are some suggestions:

1. If possible, block off the dog's access to the piece of furniture. Bedroom doors can be closed, baby

gates can be installed, or the dog can be placed in an enclosure.

2. When at home, rigidly enforce the "Off" rule, not allowing any access to furniture. Over time, this may modify the dog's view of acceptable nap locations.

3. Use deterrent devices ("scat" mats) to discourage the dog from helping herself at will. Products are available that can be laid on sofa or chair cushions that discourage jumping up by emitting a safe, low-grade electric current.

• Nuisance Barking •

While some dogs do tend to be more noisy than others, the truth is that non-stop barking is usually a sign of boredom, frustration or loneliness. The solution here is not to simply slap a bark collar on the dog. On the contrary, it should involve getting the dog more exercise, more one-on-one constructive bonding, and training the dog so she can be left inside the house rather than outside and alone.

Nuisance barking can also be a result of owners doubling as perpetual playmates/entertainers for the dogs. The dog learns, as does a small child, that the persistently "squeaky wheel eventually gets the grease". Many years ago, I had a client whose dog barked incessantly when put into the crate. To keep her quiet, he would pass her a pig's ear. He couldn't understand why the barking was getting louder and more persistent with time??

As much as possible, learn to refuse the dog's otherwise rude demand for your attention. A dog who jumps at her owner's legs, paws incessantly at your lap, or plants herself in front of you, barking as though she were "scolding" you, is *not* politely requesting your attention. In all likelihood, she has learned that sheer persistence will ultimately get her what she desires. In these situations, although it takes diligence and rock-solid resolve, the best solution is for the owner to learn how not to be manipulated. Practice simply ignoring the behavior when the dog "demands" your attention. Play the passive/aggressive approach, even denying eye contact, or walking out of the room. This nearly always works, but how quickly is dependent on the personality of the dog and/or how long the behavior has been in place. Rarely does it disappear overnight.

Some other suggested remedies for nuisance barking are:

1. Turn firmly and quickly at the dog, directing full eye contact at them. Give a stern, sharp and confident "No!" You might even want to take one assertive step toward the dog as well. Proceed to the passive/aggressive approach, ignoring the dog.

2. Use the vinegar and water squirt, aimed for the nose, to add more "drama". Use a "No!" along with the squirt. Follow up with passive/ aggressive. Repeat squirt if needed.

3. Try Level 2 Scruff Hold (Chapter 4) while you tell the dog "No!" Ignore the dog until he calms down.

4. If barking is an *outside* behavior, a "shaker can" could be effective. Fill an empty, rinsed out aluminum can with a handful of pebbles or pennies. Tape securely shut with duct tape. When barking occurs, step quickly into the vicinity of the dog, shaking the can vigorously with a stern "No!" The sudden and unnatural sound will alert the startle reflex in the dog, hopefully deterring and stopping the behavior. It must be done with consistency, catching the behavior and thwarting it as often as possible.

5. For *extreme* cases, where all other remedies have been exhausted, bark collars are available. However, research is recommended, as some are more humane and/or effective than others.

▪ Destructive Digging ▪

Make *sure* the dog has a sufficient and constructive physical outlet every day, before determining whether this is an actual problem. A lot of dogs dig out of sheer boredom, frustration or loneliness. Then again, there are certain breeds where digging is innate to the dog— Huskies, Malamutes, and many hounds. With these types of breeds, completely breaking the dog of the behavior may be more difficult. Therefore it's suggested that the owner find ways to simply *prevent* it. For instance, placing a dog into an enclosed run on a concrete slab will certainly stop digging 100%. Other preventative measures might include keeping the dog's nails trimmed very short. The encouraging thing about destructive digging, is that, with some basic persistence from the owner, most dogs outgrow the tendency.

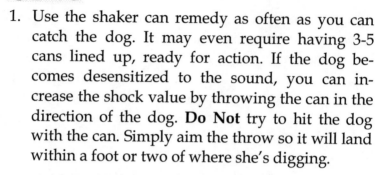

1. Use the shaker can remedy as often as you can catch the dog. It may even require having 3-5 cans lined up, ready for action. If the dog becomes desensitized to the sound, you can increase the shock value by throwing the can in the direction of the dog. **Do Not** try to hit the dog with the can. Simply aim the throw so it will land within a foot or two of where she's digging.

2. If the digging is primarily occurring at the base of trees and shrubs, or landscaped areas, try sprinkling the area generously with crushed red pepper. This is completely natural, but does have a potent kick to it if the dog stirs up the soil by digging. Commercial products are also available that emit an odor that the dog finds objectionable. Reapply the product regularly, depending on weather and moisture conditions.

3. For more intense digging (tunneling) that occurs along fence lines, making a solid perimeter of brick or concrete will make it much more difficult for the dog.

• Mouthing/Biting •

Usually seen during times of high energy and playfulness, also during some greeting rituals with owners, when petting is involved.

1. First rule is to learn how to defuse energy to at least a controllable level *before* the owners attempts to pet the dog. Follow passive/aggressive suggestions listed above under "Jumping Up". Do not attempt to pet the dog again for several

minutes, even upwards of an hour in some cases. Wait to see when the *dog* indicates she is ready. Often she will come back "asking" politely for attention, sidling up with tail down and ears slightly back.

2. When petting, offer hand palm up, then reach *below* the dog's chin. This allows the dog to see the person's hand almost the entire time, keeping many dogs calmer and under control. Reaching over the top of the dog's head (as many people do) passes the hand beyond the dog's visual range and simulates a dominance gesture. As a result, she will naturally lift her head up, open her mouth and "follow" the hand, just to keep it within view. If the dog is excited, or at a "first time" greeting, this will more than likely lead to some mouthing or nipping.

3. Sometimes offering an "alternative" to chew on (a toy or bone) is appropriate, but only *after* the owner has conveying disapproval over having their *hand* used as a chew toy.

4. If you have a very determined "player", try a Level 2 Scruff Shake or Scruff Hold for a little more forceful message, always using a firm "No!" in conjunction with the correction. Follow up with passive/aggressive approach, ignoring the dog for a period of time.

▪ Destructive Chewing ▪

Chewing is a natural behavior with dogs and should be allowed and even encouraged to a degree

to develop sound jaws and teeth, especially during teething (4-6 months). When selecting chew toys try to find ones that will keep the dog's attention *and* provide a good workout for the jaws. Soft plush toys and squeaky toys do nothing for teeth and jaw development. Real bones are okay, but be alert to any signs of food guarding aggression. Stand firm and do not allow the dog to become possessive. For more direct suggestions with this, read the chapter on "Aggression".

While it is recommended that an owner provide the dog with access to acceptable chewing items, be careful not to *overdo* it. Strewing toys and play things all over the house or back yard can send the wrong message and do more harm than good. Too many toys can over stimulate the dog, sending the message that any and all chewing is okay. I suggest leaving no more than two durable chew items within reach at any one time. Furthermore, chewing is an activity that demands supervision from a human—at least for awhile.

When my oldest female German Shepherd was a puppy she didn't exhibit excessive chewing tendencies. While she was always provided with a bone, it was never her favorite thing to do. At 8 months of age she had never once tried to chew anything *but* the bone. Thinking we were "in the clear" with her, we let our guard down. One evening when I was out with clients, my husband was home with the pup. Supervision was minimal—we felt she was trustworthy. Imagine my shock when I came home to find she had chewed up the cornice of our antique mahogany piano! Moral of the story: supervise the chewing.

All this being said, should you catch the dog trying out the furniture, a rug, the baseboard molding, or your shoes (with or without you being in them) here are some suggestions:

1. Use the vinegar and water squirt (Chapter 2, Crate Introduction) at the dog's nose with a firm "No!" at the moment the chewing begins. If you can, quickly pass an acceptable chew item towards him.

2. Grab the leash that's attached to him and give a firm Level 1 collar correction with the "No!" Pass an acceptable chew toy if you wish.

3. For particularly aggressive chewers, if the first two suggestions don't work, grab the dog by the scruff and give a firm and confident Scruff Shake, using a deep, authoritative voice along with the "No!"

4. With any and all of these suggestions, follow up with a passive/aggressive approach, ignoring the dog for a few minutes. Even walk away if you must.

5. Finally, while this suggestion doesn't strictly address *chewing*, instead, it channels the dog with an alternative activity: place the dog into a good, long, Sit/Stay (5+ minutes). This will likely calm the dog down, and by the time the Sit/Stay is over with, hopefully, he may have forgotten about chewing—at least for the moment.

• Stealing •

Two types of "stealing" will be addressed. First, stealing articles from around the house—ostensibly to get a reaction from somebody, usually due to boredom. And, second, stealing food.

Dog's can steal items around the house for various reasons. Sometimes it is due to boredom, and the dog simply is looking for something to do. Other times, it is done to test the social boundaries, as well as creating a playful challenge. Sometimes it is pure and simple curiosity. And then I've also seen dogs selectively choose an article that belongs to a specific member of the family. When my husband and I first got married, I'm sure my Springer Spaniel felt slighted. He was used to getting all my attention with no competition. Not an aggressive dog by nature, he showed his disapproval by selectively removing my husband's socks and underwear from the laundry hamper and hiding them in his bedding. When I went to retrieve them, it was obvious he had taken out his frustrations on these articles of clothing.

First determine *what* has been stolen, and then, if possible, *why*. Your response to the incident will be determined by the "why" part. If you think the dog is bored, take the item away calmly, then give her something to do. Suggestions might be a long Sit/Stay next to you, some quick Down/Up sequences, or even a short walk if possible. You might pass a toy to the dog *after* the aforementioned exercises, so that it doesn't appear immediately as though you are rewarding the stealing.

If you think the dog is playfully testing you, try to avoid getting into a physical altercation with the dog--that may be one of the dog's angles as well (rough-housing or tug-of-war). Determine *what* has been taken, and decide whether it's valuable enough to bother with. Many people succeed in reducing the occurrence of thievery by using reverse psychology. After all, the "value" of an item, to some degree, is based on how much *others* might desire it as well. Sometimes, if the dog sees you don't care, or that he can't "get a rise out of you", he may likely stop the behavior. If, on the other hand, the article *is* of value, at least control the situation by not reacting with so much emotion. Calmly tell the dog to Sit. Slowly walk toward the dog and calmly give the "release" command. Praise the dog verbally. *Do not* pass a treat to the dog for this. It will encourage him to repeat the behavior because he has been *too* rewarded. Do some constructive mental exercises if you wish.

Curiosity as a reason for thievery is something that most dogs outgrow with age. Keep the dog under supervision and leave a leash on him. Correct with mild corrections if needed, passing the dog an acceptable item once you have retrieved what was in his mouth.

If you've got a dog who is purposefully selecting only items belonging to a specific member of the family, try to get that person more involved in the training and interaction with the dog. Sometimes this isn't possible--for instance when the "specific member of the family" is a new baby. If this is the case, keep the dog with you under supervision and control when the baby is around. The dog needs to learn calm, submissive behavior around this defenseless member of the pack. Most dogs adjust to new babies within 1-2 months. Nevertheless, this last example of stealing may be a manifestation of some social turmoil in the dog that should be addressed. My Springer, for instance, got over his resentment of my husband quickly after Kevin took him for a few walks and took over the feeding of the dog.

Stealing food can be a little trickier to correct, as most dogs figure out rapidly *not* to try it when humans are around. Thus there is the added frustration of lack of trust and sneakiness as well. Here are some suggestions that, if implemented *early on* in the training, may help reduce the dog's overall curiosity:

1. When eating, keep the dog across the room, at least 8 feet away. You can even opt for placing her into a Sit/Stay command.

2. Make no eye contact with the dog during the entire meal.

3. **Do not** offer the dog any "people" food.

4. When cooking in the kitchen, establish boundaries, keeping the dog out of the room

5. Work on gradual desensitizing exercises, placing the dog on a Sit/Stay and stepping out of sight for 10-20 seconds. Work the exercise as directed in Chapter 6 (Hidden Stay) building up the dog's tolerance and reliability.

6. With children or babies, rigidly adhere to suggestion 1, and discourage children from eating food while walking from room to room.

For larger dogs who are "counter cruisers" — dog's who scan kitchen counters — learn to be fastidious and clean up immediately when you're finished preparing something. For smaller dogs, keep chairs pushed all the way in at tables and bar counters so the chairs cannot be used as a "launch pad". For extreme cases, some people have had success using a cat deterrent pad. These are very low voltage electrically charged rubber surfaces that can be laid on furniture, floor areas and the like. When touched, the sensation is a prickly feeling, similar to static.

Stealing of cat food is also very common. Dogs just seem to find it irresistible. If the dog in question is a smaller breed, placing the cat food up out of reach is probably the best and easiest solution. Cats are great jumpers and it won't be any hardship for "kitty" to have to jump onto the laundry room counter to get her food. Securing the door partially open to allow room just for the cat can work, as well as installing a small cat door into the food room. If you have a dog the same size as or smaller than the cat, these last two suggestions wouldn't necessarily work. There are also inexpensive signaling or alarm devises that can act as a deterrent as well.

▪Submissive or Excitement Urination▪

This is not the same as general house-training. In both cases (submissive or excited) the dog is acting

almost unconsciously. Submissive urination is a defense mechanism. It is observed in situations when a timid and/or younger dog meets an older or higher ranking individual. In displays of either active or passive submission, a small amount of urine may pass, increasing the scent odor of the encounter. It is also common in cases of abuse or excessively physical handling, where the dog may develop a hypersensitivity to any and all corrections—even a raised voice. The solution in these cases is to approach training with calmness and sensitivity. Avoid extremes in your conduct toward the dog—whether that be excessive affection or coddling, or stern corrections. What these cases typically require is developing the dog's self-confidence in a consistent and predictable environment. Never correct a dog for submissive urination. It makes it worse!

Excitement urination is simply the result of weak bladder muscles that give way during moments of great enthusiasm. Ever laughed so hard you peed your pants? It's fairly similar. This, like submissive urination, is not a condition that requires a "correction". The easiest solution is to address the emotional state that is the catalyst for the peeing. When the dog is extremely excited (during an emotionally unbridled greeting, for instance) try simply ignoring her. Doubling the dog's enthusiasm with *your* response may be all that's needed for the bladder to fail. In general, encourage calm self-control until the dog's muscles develop more strength with time and maturity.

•Eating Feces•

The 25 cent word for this is *coprophagia,* and there are many theories about why dogs will investigate and consume their own or another animals feces. None of the explanations will necessarily make owners feel any better about the behavior, and it is quite likely to cause a health condition in the dog if allowed to persist. Here are some ideas about why it occurs:

1. Simple curiosity. To a dog, feces carry a lot of interesting odors, telling about the animal and their diet. Part of a dog's method of exploration is oral.

2. Instinctive behavior. Bitches stimulate elimination in the new pups by licking the genitals. As a result, they also consume the waste. Survival may depend on reducing the smells that could attract predators.

3. Hiding odors. This is an extension of the preceding item. Sometimes it appears that higher ranking dogs will consume the feces of lower ranking members, thus leaving only their own scent as the predominant one.

4. Inadequate nutrition. This one seems to be the least plausible to me with the exception of dogs who have Exocrine Pancreatic Insufficiency. With this disease, the sufferer lacks the enzyme to properly digest the food, thus nutrients are not absorbed into the system. Food literally runs right through, and even though the dogs seem to eat an enormous amount, they are actually starving to death. As a result, they will consume the feces out of desperation.

My experience has been primarily with the first and the second explanations. If the culprit is still a pup, chances are good they will outgrow the behavior, especially if the owners are conscientious about cleaning up the bathroom area and keeping the dog away from feces. There are products available that can deter consumption of feces, some are more effective than others. Talk to your veterinarian. Unfortunately, some dogs are just die-hard stool eaters. I have had some students who owned dogs that, no matter what they tried, the behavior could not be broken. That is rare, but not unheard-of.

In my experience, given the opportunity, all dogs will clean out cat boxes. As far as I can tell, this has no explanation other than they just seem to like eating it, as disgusting as that sounds. If you have this problem, take suggestions from "Stealing—cat food" (*except* putting the box on a counter) and try the same. Otherwise buy a cover for the cat box. In any case, try to be more fastidious cleaning the box at least twice a day, or purchase a self-cleaning cat box.

•Children and Dogs•

Statistically, children, as a group, suffer the worst in encounters with dogs. Between the ages of 0-4 years, children are far more likely than an adult to have a bad altercation with a dog, from a minor bite, to a fatal mauling. The reasons are varied, but certainly one of the most obvious facts is that these victims, as a group, are completely vulnerable to dogs. Furthermore, if a child does get bitten by a dog, they are far more likely to scream, thrash and panic than is an adult, all of which can escalate the intensity of the encounter from the dog's perspective. Young boys between the ages of 2 and 4 are also statistically more likely to be the victim than are young girls. Risking a stereotype of young boys and their play patterns, but a loud, energetic young boy is more likely to elicit rambunctious, physical behavior from a dog. Pointing and waving sticks is a common play pattern for many young boys.

Children in this age group are also unable, with their cognitive development, to recognize any aggressive displays a dog might be sending, attempting to warn them off.

This is not at all to say that dogs and children can't be good combinations, or that they can't mutually benefit from the relationship. Nothing could be further from the truth. However, parents and adults need to strictly supervise interaction. As soon as the child is old enough to comprehend, parents should instruct them on respectful behavior and interaction with the dog. All too often, children view and treat dogs as stuffed animals,

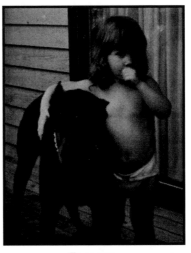

▪ JEWEL ▪

Photography: Kevin Neary

offering excessive physical attention, big bear hugs and other "investigative" type behavior; i.e. pulling of legs, tails and ears. Some dogs are infinitely patient with

this (an old female Doberman Pinscher I had years ago would lay placidly while our infant son crawled over her) while others are not. Many dogs are downright nervous around children, making their anxiety known with barking, quivering, tucked tails and attempts to flee. Forcing such dogs into encounters with children before the dog is ready will only lead to more problems.

Teaching children from an early age how to conduct themselves calmly around dogs and puppies will help immensely. Teach children the basics about dog body language, game playing and personal space—all major culprits in child/dog interaction. Involving young children in some basic canine care giving and maintenance can expand their awareness of the needs of this being, as well as teaching responsibility. With adult supervision to begin with, I especially recommend having children in charge of the daily feeding. (See the section on "Feeding Ritual" in this chapter.) Not only does this give a great degree of satisfaction to children, but is a simple exercise that can help set the child above the dog in rank—in control of a much needed resource.

▪Separation Anxiety▪

This is an all-too-common problem with dogs. Destruction and damage as a result of this state of panic can be enormous. My in-laws had a dog that chewed a hole right through a door trying to get out. Years ago, a male German Shepherd of mine gnawed the corner right off the bottom stair, carpet and all. Some dogs will claw at a door until their pads are torn to shreds.

Some students of mine with two Whippets were greeted after work, day after day, with the mess of diarrhea brought on from separation anxiety.

Dogs will naturally and instinctively pack up. Within this pack there is security, strength and identity. Separation from that pack, then, becomes an unnatural and possibly frightening event. Dogs may wander off solo, following something of curiosity, but the purpose of their venture is certainly not to become lost or permanently separated from their group. When a dog realizes he is lost, a sense of panic can easily set in, as isolation is seen as a threat to his security. Lone dogs are more vulnerable.

By bringing a dog into the home, people create a surrogate pack with their canine friend, giving them a stable environment. Once the bond is created, dogs will stick with their owners like a true pack, seeking shelter and security. Consequently, separation from their owners, just like from a pack of dogs, can trigger anxiety and fear just as readily. The dog does not project eight hours in the future when the owner will be returning home from work. There is only the moment — and the moment says "abandonment".

Separation Anxiety (SA) is not limited to timid, shy dogs. It can just as easily be a problem with dogs who seem to have great social confidence. Much of it may stem from how solid the social structure is between dog and owner. Making sure the proper hierarchy has been established with owner as leader should be part of the solution. Dogs who view themselves as "leaders"

WOOF DID YOU SAY? ■

in the relationship can be more prone to act out when left alone. In such cases, the dog may see isolation as a neglect of the human's duties to leave the "leader" behind. Years ago, a student related how life with her previous Bichon Frisé had been a nightmare. According to neighbors' reports, the dog would bark all day, every day, while the owner was at work. The barking only ceased when she came home. Some simple questions about the relationship that existed between the two revealed that the dog was very spoiled, and used to being pampered and entertained. It was not uncommon for the owner, out of a sense of guilt, to bring home special toys or treats as an "apology". A couple hours every night, as well, were spent entertaining and playing with the dog. Rarely did the dog get walked. As the relationship grew, the dog became increasingly demanding, until the behavior reached it's highest level, a combination of unmet physical needs (no exercise) and a convoluted sense of duties. The owner was the follower, serving the every need of the king (dog).

This is not to say that people should quit their jobs or get work-from-home positions to satisfy their dogs. Being able to handle separation is something dogs can learn, but it should be taught gently and with patience and understanding. Some dogs seem to have little to no problem with it. Others, due to personality types or past experiences, suffer near total mental meltdowns.

Separation Anxiety can be greatly reduced if an owner uses a crate. However, it should never be

■ 245 ■

presented in a threatening manner, potentially causing a dog to panic when placed in it. Read in Chapter 2 about how to introduce a crate properly. Since
SA can be alleviated by using a crate, it makes sense to
introduce it in a natural and non-threatening manner.

Some other suggestions for helping to reduce
Separation Anxiety are:

1. Make sure the dog has had some good exercise
    before you leave. She will be more relaxed, possi-
    bly even take a nap while you're out. I recom-
    mend this especially as a morning regimen, giv-
    ing the dog a short, brisk walk *before* you leave
    for work. This may not be easy to fit in, but the
    benefits are worth the effort. After all, waiting 8+
    hours for your walk is hard for any dog.

2. Read Chapter 2 about introducing a crate. Make
    sure it is used at times even though someone may
    be in the house.

3. Start small. Step out just for short spurts at first,
    maybe just 10-15 minutes. Even "feigning" a de-
    parture is not altogether unreasonable. It allows
    you to secretly monitor the dog, allowing for quick
    responses if you sense or hear him panicking.

4. Don't respond out of guilt. Don't overdo it on the
    good-byes when you leave, or the hellos when you
    return. Be calm and in control, encouraging the dog
    to pick up on your confident, relaxed manner.

5. Leave on a radio or the television, set to some-
    thing calm and soothing.

6. If possible, have a friend or neighbor come over
    and let the dog out half-way through the day.

See if they can take the dog for a short walk. Whether this be a friend, or a professional dog-walker, explain the agenda and try to get them to reinforce the calm, controlled approach as well.

7. Work diligently on the Hidden Stay exercises in Chapter 6, getting him used to spending time alone, even though you may be in the house.

8. Know your dog's personality type intimately and work within it. Accentuate his strengths, and work to overcome his weaknesses.

9. If you have a timid dog, be more patient and set more reasonable, long-term goals.

10. Consider getting a second dog for a companion. Studies have proven that having another animal around (it might even be a cat) can help a dog relax. However, since adding another animal adds more work for the owner, it is recommended that the preceding suggestions be tried *first,* before going with a companion animal.

When teaching and conditioning the dog not to panic when left alone, the best exercises are those that are sensitive to the dog's per-

A companion may alleviate Separation Anxiety.
Photo courtesy of Bennett & Hastings

spective. Look for long term goals, built on gentle and gradual desensitizing of the dog to being left alone. Some former students related a story regarding separation anxiety. They had been directed by a previous trainer to leave the dog alone in another room, barricading her in and giving no forewarning of their impending exit. They were then told to go one or two rooms away and *stay away*, regardless of the dog's loud and agonizing reaction, until her violent emotion subsided. At that point they were to return, thus teaching the dog that her desire (reunion with the pack) was only fulfilled when she was calm.

This may eventually have worked, but at what cost psychologically to the dog? Stay away from exercises that are so emotionally intense or demanding that they create more anxiety/problems on their own. Technically, SA is *not* an obedience problem. It is a psychological issue that is handled best with re-conditioning techniques. Using "corrections" for destructive behavior generated from intense emotions usually doesn't help. In fact, it often heightens the unpleasantness of the associations and the situation in the dog's mind. Being sensitive to this and understanding the root causes of the issue will help the owner design the best approach for their individual dog.

CHAPTER 8

AGGRESSION

This part of a dog's nature makes most people cringe, step back in shock and fear, have sweaty palms, etc. Some people claim

Image courtesy Bennett & Hastings

that we can *never* trust dogs. There are an estimated 53 million dogs in this country alone (my guess is it's much higher). If dog aggression really was such a serious issue, I doubt people would continue to share their homes so readily with these creatures. The truth is, that serious incidents of aggression (resulting in major bites requiring medical attention, or even death) are phenomenally small considering the amount of contact we have with dogs on a daily basis. It might be that dogs are far more patient with *us* than the other way around. Unfortunately, when these incidents do occur, they receive massive media coverage, creating panic and sometimes a knee-jerk response to ban breeds and/or pass relatively ineffective dog legislation to control the problem. According to Karen Delise, "...if there is an answer to be found to the problem of severe or fatal dog bites to humans, it is to be found in the *relationship* between the two species."[1]
(emphasis added)

1. *Fatal Dog Attacks, The Stories Behind the Statistics.* Karen Delise. Anubis Press, Manorville, New York. 2002.

Although serious aggression issues with dogs are relatively small based on the entire population, it is the basis for nearly one-third of my business. I suspect that most altercations wherein someone (a person or another dog or animal) has gotten injured could have been averted or at least had reduced trauma if owners were more tuned in to "reading" the warning signs. As mentioned in Chapter 3, where dog body language was discussed, dogs will *always* signal their intentions.* There are no cases of normal, healthy dogs acting out a true "Jekyll and Hyde" scenario. Even that well-known literary image, though, is unfair, because Dr. Jekyll *did* actually drink a solution that caused his transformation. This is not to say that an owner will have unlimited time to read and respond to the signals. At times, there may be a delay of a few seconds. Other times, it may only be a blink of an eye. Because of this, it is critical to always be aware of the dog's body language, especially when in public places.

Unfortunately, humans are, for the most part, woefully inept at recognizing the signs of impending aggression, or taking appropriate steps to prevent potential conflict. One morning, when walking with two of my German Shepherds, I noticed a woman about a block away with her two dogs. One was an older, male, Golden Retriever. The other was a smaller breed, possibly a Pekinese mix. Both dogs were on retractable leashes, several feet from their

*The only exception to this is a behavior called "Springer Rage", wherein the dog seems to lack any ability to signal.. Attacks seem to come out of the blue. It is still not "normal" behavior, and only a very small percentage of dogs seem to do this anyway.

owner. The woman noticed me on approach, as did her dogs. Her Golden took on an immediate "challenge" position, planting himself directly in our path, body rigid, tail erect, eyes frozen on my dogs in a direct stare. In an attempt to avert a confrontation, I stepped into the street as we passed by. The Golden remained thus, (his owner woefully ignorant of his intentions) until we got within 10 feet, at which point he lunged forward in an aggressive attack. Thankfully, no harm was done, and no fight ensued. The point of this story is that for a full 20 seconds or more, this particular dog had been signaling his intentions. Had the owner been aware of her dog and/or these signals, there would have been plenty of time to react and redirect him. Sadly, it is too often the case that people misread the dog, or are simply ignorant to dog language.

Unfortunately, denial is also common when owners see their dogs displaying aggression. As with children, we don't like to admit that our own children could ever be capable of breaking the law or doing something dangerous to others. That's "the other guy's kid" that does that. I'm sure the woman with the Golden Retriever was completely taken off guard—after all, Golden Retrievers are generally regarded as having docile temperaments. Truth is, every dog that walks the planet is capable of aggression, given the right set of circumstances. All that is needed in many situations is the right catalyst. Because aggressive behavior from dogs is a serious liability and safety issue, it should never be taken lightly. Being honest with yourself as well your dog's potential must be part of the solution.

Aggression is not limited to specific breeds. We seem to take immediate notice of aggressive behavior with large, stereotypically "mean" breeds of dogs, and then paradoxically (and hypocritically) ignore identical displays with small breeds. Many trainers and handlers will admit to being bitten far more often from small, high energy breeds than from large ones. This might very likely be a result of vastly different handling from owners, coupled with the dog's already high strung temperament. Small dogs are notoriously pampered and spoiled, often just *because* of their size. They seem to draw out an innate human instinct to protect and nurture something ostensibly smaller and more fragile. The true paradox, however, is that the dog does not see himself as being small and fragile. Since dogs have no self-awareness, treating one dog differently from another solely due to size is a gross misapplication of philosophy and understanding of dog behavior. Within only a .2% range in DNA, dogs are genetically identical in make-up. Furthermore, the excuse that "small dogs can't do as much harm/damage" is indefensible when looked at from the perspective of a child. The psychological trauma sustained from a bite can be just as severe and long lasting as the physical trauma. Owners should realize and acknowledge that the impetus for aggressive behavior is exactly the same, regardless of a dog's size or breed.

Social skills, or the lack of them, is a common cause of aggressive episodes. Owners often fail to expose their dogs to enough of the many intricacies of human social existence, or varied contact with

other dogs. Unless an owner actually does live a completely reclusive life, there will always be things that will challenge the dog's sense of stability and security. In Chapter 3, the case of the Chihuahua was a classic example of inadequate socialization, coupled with a fragile social structure being threatened by me, the trainer. This dog's behavior was primarily generated through fear, as he saw his world crumbling around him.

Other cases of aggression brought on by lack of socialization can be generated by the opposite emotional motivation—dominance and assertion of rank. Dogs who "rule the roost" at home, and are limited in their exposure to the wide array of other temperaments, can easily develop a bully mentality. An attitude of being able to "push everybody around" is easy to build if the owners are always bending to the whim of the dog—no rules or any consistent adherence to them. The dog learns that aggression serves his needs and allows him (in a very primitive fashion) to control his environment. Unfortunately, carrying that same attitude into the real world is bound to cause problems, as there will invariably be another dog who is more assertive than he. Not teaching a dog the fine art of diplomacy and compromise can bring about problems just as well.

In all this discussion, remember that "an ounce of prevention is worth a pound of cure". In other words, taking the initiative to train, educate and socialize the dog right from the start will do a world of good to *prevent* any behaviors from escalating into aggressive displays. Be pro-active in dealing with the dog, rather than re-active. And, above all, be *consistent,* even after the "lessons" are over. Occasionally I receive calls from former students who are experiencing aggression problems. After some fact-finding, the most common denominators in these cases are too much relaxation of the rules, coupled with a slow, steady decline in the owner's vigilance and awareness of passive messaging. Most of these people are unaware that this steady erosion of their authority is taking place. Consequently, it is quite a shock when they are suddenly confronted with a snarling dog.

Aggressive *displays* are part of the natural repertoire of language between dogs. In *Dog Language, An Encyclopedia of Canine Behavior,* Roger Abrantes states that "Aggression is a drive—purposeful energy—which is aroused by meeting with a **conspecific.** (fellow dog). Conspecifics compete over vital resources... Aggression is the drive behind the initial desire of one individual to kill another, or preferably chase it away... However, other animals have realized that they need help from conspecifics to survive... This does not mean aggression disappears, rather it assumes other forms through ritualized behavior: greeting ceremonies, pacifying behavior and rank ordering."[2] Aggressive displays, thus, are just as much a part of the communication process as any other. While it may be, in some situations, the most dramatic way to resolve conflict or control a situation, it is effective to

2. *Dog Language, An Encyclopedia of Canine Behaviour.* Wakan Tanka Publishers. 1997. Distributed by DogWise, Wenatchee, Wash. pg. 37

some degree. The key is to prevent the emotion from which it is generated from getting out of hand, thus creating an unpleasant physical altercation. Unfortunately, most humans react out of shock, fear, or frustration, often because they "didn't see it coming". But reacting out of *fear*, as many owners do, can escalate and intensify the emotion of the encounter. Consider the following case:

A couple with a terrier mix came to me because of what appeared, to them, to be unusually high levels of aggression directed toward other dogs. In spite of many veterinarians telling them "terriers are just like that", common sense encouraged these folks to seek assistance. Upon observation of the dog, it became apparent that there were a number of issues all battling together. First, the dog wasn't getting sufficient exercise or psychological/mental direction. Rules were inconsistent or nonexistent. This terrier also had little contact with other dogs. (Due to his aggressive outbursts, the owners were decidedly apprehensive about playmates.) When he encountered another dog, the reaction was an astonishing combination of fear, territorial aggression and intra-species aggression, stemming from underdeveloped social skills. The owners would then typically yank and/or restrain the dog, raising their voices and otherwise add to the stress of the encounter. Eventually they would just drag the dog away as fast as they could, perpetuating a thoroughly unproductive pattern of behavior.

After several weeks of steady training, we felt the dog was ready for his first "off-leash" encounter with another member of his species. I brought my oldest female GSD—calm and confident, patient but not a push-over. When the dogs were first released into the area, the terrier made a bee-line toward my German Shepherd. As Lily (my dog) stood her ground, the terrier froze, unsure of himself. For a couple seconds there was a stare-down, and then the terrier lunged quickly at Lily's scruff. The wife reacted instantly, taking a step toward her dog and drawing her breath in audibly. I quickly got her to relax and wait. Another couple seconds passed as Lily just stood patiently, waiting for the terrier to let go. No fighting developed, the dogs relaxed as well, and were soon running around the enclosure, chasing and playing. Over the course of about half and hour, there were very few tense encounters, and without the humans jumping in with more negative energy, the dogs learned to let it pass, adapt and move on. The happiest part of this story is that Grrr (the terrier) now attends doggy day-care twice a week, enjoying contact with a variety of dogs.

• TYPES OF AGGRESSION •

All types of aggression serve a purpose to some degree. Dogs carry the same basic instincts to respond in a given environment. Whether one dog chooses to react where another one won't is initially due to temperament, personality and breed tendency. When humans enter the picture, we add training and socialization as reasons as well. It is easier to understand aggression if we categorize it based on the environments or situations that trigger it. Having this information is critical to planning a

solution. Much of the work involved in treating aggression issues boils down to teaching a dog other, more socially constructive ways of dealing with frustration or stress. It can involve reorienting a dog's perspective, reconstructing a more effective social hierarchy, developing greater social skills, and/or more effectively controlling the environment that triggers the behavior. Also required is the careful and attentive involvement of the owner, learning to *read the signals* and being alert to the beginning stages of the behavior.

The following are, broadly speaking, the major types or categories of dog aggression:

1. Defensive (fear) Aggression:
   an emotional over-reaction to a situation, flight reaction

2. Dominance Aggression:
   assertion of rank to impose the will of one over another

3. Intra-Sexual Aggression:
   within the same gender; male-to-male, female-to-female.

4. Parental Aggression:
   instinctive behavior to protect the young

5. Possessive Aggression:
   guarding of items, i.e. toys, food, etc.

6. Predatory Aggression:
   related to prey or hunt drive, to chase moving objects

7. Territorial Aggression:
   defending of territory, as in house, yard, car, etc.

Some aggressive displays are *combinations* of more than one type—Grr the terrier, for instance.

Other times, one type can flow into another. A dog senses a cat on the other side of the fence. He reacts initially with Territorial Aggression, asserting his turf to the intruder. As the cat (quite foolishly) jumps to the top of the fence, the motivation switches in the blink of an eye to Predatory Aggression, as the dog lunges forward in an attempt to catch the animal.

With each of the categories of aggression, its function in a natural state will be given. While all of the types of aggression are instinctive within the dog, some carry an aspect of *learned* behavior as well. That is critical, as *learned* behavior usually can be *re-learned*. Completely instinctive behaviors, on the other hand, are far more difficult to eliminate. Common triggers to each behavior will be listed, and then suggested solutions to each will be offered, in order of effectiveness, based on the *intensity* of the display and the dog's stage of learning.

Be aware of variations in breed specific behavior throughout this discussion. Do not assume that one dog/breed will display any particular type of behavior to the degree or in exactly the same manner as another. This is *not* an excuse for excessive or inappropriate aggressive behavior, but rather a realistic expectation of what a dog is bred for. For instance, with my own GSD's, I expect (and generally get) some predictable level of territorial and dominance aggression. That is specifically bred into German Shepherds. I would be sorely disappointed if one of my dogs displayed the easy-going, all-friendly disposition of a Cavalier King Charles Spaniel, for instance. That is

not to say that I allow their behavior to get out-of-hand. But, it would be grossly unfair of me to insist they be total "pussy-cats" in certain situations. Do not set unrealistic goals for your dog or breed.

One other type of aggression that is often talked about (it is not on the list) is "leash" aggression. Owners that experience this describe it as very assertive, dominant or bully-like behavior when their dog sees another animal when walking on a leash. The term "leash" aggression, is a misrepresentation of what is actually happening. In most of these cases, the leash is actually a source of *frustration*, as the dog (who often hasn't learned sufficiently how to handle a "No, you can't have that") sees something that he desires—often another dog. As his enthusiasm and excitement increase, the owner often applies more and more tension on the leash. This does nothing to draw the dog's attention away from the other animal, in fact, is serves only to frustrate and possibly anger the dog. When it reaches a breaking point, the dog begins to lunge, bark, snap, etc., possibly even misdirecting the behavior at the unwitting owner.

Ty, a Chow/Border Collie cross would typically get excited when on a walk if he saw another dog. Being strong-willed and assertive by his personality and temperament, he would begin pulling toward the other dog. Initial greeting behavior was typified by assertive and dominance type posturing, often intimidating the other dog. It was not unusual for the greeting to then escalate into Ty attempting an aggressive pounce onto the other dog. As the owners became more disturbed by the behavior, they limited and eventually tried to completely prevent Ty from going up to any other dogs. This, unfortunately, did not make the situation better. In fact, it made it worse, as Ty now became frustrated. Collar corrections escalated the frustration, and at times he did turn an angry growl toward the owners.

The solution to this case was more involved than just doing basic socialization and leash work. In order to get Ty to look to his owners for guidance and direction, we had to first restructure the social hierarchy, making sure the dog knew he was not the one making the decisions. The owners were taught, over several weeks, to calmly and steadily use passive messaging coupled with obedience exercises to change Ty's perspective.

• Defensive (Fear) Aggression •

This type of aggression is the result of the dog being denied access to his "flight" response to a perceived threat. In a natural state, the two options for the dog when he feels under attack or vulnerable, are "fight or flight". If one is removed, the dog will naturally access the other in a pinch. This is an instinctive reaction in the dog—a matter of survival—at least as far as he sees it. Physical indicators will be lowered (even tucked) tails, tightly drawn back ears, brows and eyes pulled back, and weight shifted slightly back. Lips can also be drawn tightly back revealing teeth and gum line.

Defensive aggression is probably the most common reason why people get bitten by dogs. The dog feels "backed into a corner", and the "intruder" continues to push forward. Time and time again, people do not read the dog's signals. How often does it happen that, when greeting a dog, the human thrusts themselves abruptly into the dog's personal space with an outstretched hand? If the dog is shy or fearful, this is *not* seen as a friendly gesture. That's the *human* translation. When a dog is ready to say "Hello", *he* will generally initiate the approach, not the other way around.

Since these situations are generated by extreme emotion, the use of any type of physical correction is usually ineffective, and can even do more harm than good. As stated earlier in the book, specific "corrections" are given to dogs who are experiencing a *normal range* of emotion. Correcting a dog for fear-generated behavior may just push him over the edge. On the reverse, though, neither should the owner respond directly to the dog's emotional state by petting, soothing or protecting the dog. Since petting equates as praise/approval, an owner is unwittingly reinforcing the fear by playing the parental role.

Depending on the intensity of the fear, using food to re-condition the dog may also be ineffective. When a dog shuts down emotionally to his surroundings, it can be *total*. In a sense, he *becomes* the fear, and is completely oblivious to his surroundings. Psychologically the dog is unresponsive to his

environment, seeking only a place of shelter, away from the object of fear.

The single most important thing an owner can do to reduce to incidence of Defensive Aggression is to *thoroughly socialize* the dog. Start as early as you can, and take the dog out in public as often as possible. Practice good manners, and broaden the dog's awareness of life around him. A dog that has "been around the block" a few times will be much less likely to overreact to a situation.

When a dog is in a state of fear, the best course of action is to get him to re-direct his attention *away* from the fear object. This does not mean hurrying the dog away from the fear object or situation. If there has been enough training done that the owner feels they can, in some way, control the dog *physically*, then doing some basic desensitizing exercises may be in order.

Do not try to push the dog beyond her capacity to adapt at any one time. For instance, a dog that is afraid of loud noises won't get over it quickly by being taken to the annual fireworks display on the 4th of July. *Flooding* the dog's senses isn't the same as carefully choreographed *desensitizing*. I always like the "Sit/Stay" exercise for basic desensitizing. Holding the leash and periodically reminding the dog, calmly, to "Stay", helps keep her mind split, at least partially, between focusing on the exercise and focusing on the fear object. Remain in the situation for at least 3-5 minutes if possible. Hopefully you will

begin to see a "relaxing" of the dog's body language, indicating that she is slowly working through the situation on her own. With enough practice and exposure, the dog will eventually be able to focus fully on the command, as opposed to the fear situation.

The Case of Felix and the Orange Recliner

Years ago, I owned a very easily startled male GSD. Due to illness as a pup that kept him in seclusion, he had never been sufficiently exposed at a young age to enough new experiences. Thus, he always carried with him a very suspicious and overly cautious attitude toward anything new or out of the ordinary. One morning when out walking, we encountered a bright orange recliner that a neighbor had left for pick-up at the edge of the road. The chair had not been there the last time we walked that route. Its odd size, shape and location completely took the dog off-guard. Felix immediately froze, went rigid, and then tried to back behind me. I was able, after a couple minutes, to get Felix to Heel with me past the chair. We did this many times, over the course of maybe five minutes. Each pass-by, the dog gained more confidence, until he finally stretched out his nose to cautiously sniff the chair. When he saw that this "creature" allowed him to enter its personal space without retaliating, he looked up at me, wagged his tail, and inadvertently bumped the chair with his rear-end. Of course, it moved, and thus we had to start the exercise all over again.

While Felix didn't display any classic signs of "aggression" in this situation, being fearful or suspicious of anything new is not uncommon behavior. Approach such situations with calm, repetitive exercises that build the dog's self-confidence. Forcing the dog abruptly and too quickly to adjust can trigger more dramatic fear reactions, possibly resulting in attempts to bite.

The Case of Frank the Dachshund

This young dog, like many dogs, carried feelings of apprehension regarding children. Their rapid, unpredictable movements, their loud voices, only startled and unnerved the dog. The owners took Frank to a playground to do some desensitizing work, staying cautiously at the edges of the play area, away from the most intense concentration of children. After several of these sessions, Frank began to relax, his tail even cautiously wagged a bit. After about half and hour, the owner indicated to a child that she might come over and approach the dog to pet him. Frank remained calm during the interaction. Unfortunately, though, the other children took immediate notice, and six more came running over all at once. Frank, on the end of the leash, was immediately overwhelmed and tried to get away—flight reaction. When he realized he couldn't (on the end of the leash) he actually took the other option and made one quick snap at the group of children. No one got bitten in this encounter, but it serves to underscore the importance of educating children about proper behavior around dogs.

■ Dominance Aggression ■

This type of aggression is primarily generated from a desire or need to assert rank over another as a way to control the immediate environment. It can be displayed in encounters with other dogs or people. Physical indicators can be any of the following: direct eye contact, tails lifted, ears fully forward, and weight shifted over the shoulder area. Hackles may or may not be elevated, as well as baring of teeth and/or growling. Normally, if the display goes on long enough, one dog will back down, acknowledging the higher rank and authority of the other, at least in this encounter. Once one dog backs down, the other animal usually relaxes his posturing, but often will be cautious to make sure the submissive dog continues to "watch his step".

These displays are common during initial greeting ceremonies between two dogs of at least moderate social confidence. It is also much more common between two dogs of like gender. Unaltered dogs (non-neutered) are more prone to display rank in this manner than are altered. Dominance displays can be observed between pups as young as 5 and 6 weeks old. Observable behaviors might include mounting, pawing, biting, growling, baring of teeth and even rolling each other onto the side. Pups at this stage, engaged in these games, should not be corrected. They are learning important life skills. It is also at this age that pups will learn bite inhibitions. As they interact and play with each other, they will learn when enough is enough, by the yipping and vocalizing of the other pups. When the yip reaches a certain pitch, the aggressor will generally back off. Pups that are denied interaction with other pups often do not learn this important skill. In some cases,

this can be a developing cause of dominance aggression in adulthood.

Some breeds have a greater likelihood than others of using these displays during greetings. When my own dogs first meet a new dog, their typical response is to be alert and cautious. As a rule, I monitor the dog's signals, redirecting their focus for as long as it takes until they relax. I know from experience that if intense energy during an initial encounter is allowed to flow unchecked into "free interaction", it can sometimes lead to problems. Assertive by their nature, my GSD's usually need 2-3 minutes to simply relax with a new dog before they can comfortably play.

In my experience, a large percentage of dogs who use dominance aggression in every day encounters, have had "leadership" lacking in their relationship with their owners and/or in training. If the training process does not solidly teach the dog to *look to the owner* for guidance and direction, then aggressive displays can be all too common. (Remember the case of Ty.) In homes where the dog has been spoiled and catered to, her sense of rank can easily become inflated. If there are no clear rules or boundaries that are established for acceptable behavior, then the dog can easily learn to manipulate her environment using these displays. Exercises that address the issue of "protocol" can teach dogs to defer *their* immediate needs or wishes for the *greater good of the pack*. This also teaches them constructive ways of handling minor frustrations—something life is full of.

In many cases, especially when the dog is making aggressive displays at *people*, I have found that the "nothing for free" approach can work very well. This amounts to making the dog "earn" every privilege in life: food, attention, affection, etc. For instance, before a walk, have him Sit calmly while the leash is put on. At the door going out, have him Sit again and demonstrate self-control. Make sure he Heels appropriately the entire length of the walk. Play time with others dogs is *earned* through demonstrating good behavior. Offer affection and praise *only* when he has earned it for correct behavior to a command, or is exhibiting otherwise calm behavior. (Read more about the "Affection Factor" in Chapter 3.) Hold *firmly* to any and all "passive messages" (Chapter 3) that assert your rank over the dog's. At mealtimes, follow protocol exercises, again making him Sit calmly before releasing the food to him. For more exercises on this, also see Chapter 7.

Insufficient socialization is another issue that can generate dominance aggression . Dogs who don't get enough contact and interaction with a wide variety of dogs can lack the skills needed to modify and adjust behavior to meet the situation. An owner who only allows their dog to play with a limited number of animals can thwart the social growth of their dog. This doesn't mean that play *with no boundaries* is appropriate either. But much can be gained by learning the myriad "dialects" from playing with many different types of dogs.

The Case of Shady Lady

A female, spayed Staffordshire Terrier, age 3, was nearly impossible to take for a walk around the neighborhood. Whenever another dog was encountered (and there were several on any given day) Shady's reaction was so intense that it seemed no amount of leash control could stop her in her desire to "get at" the other dog. It did not matter whether the other dog was behind a fence, visible or not, or walking on-leash with their owner. The intensity of Shady's outbursts was beyond the owner's ability to control.

At home, she lived with two other dogs: an older neutered male American Bull Dog, age 5, and a younger, spayed female Pit Bull mix. For the most part, they all got along, with the occasional "spat" between the females. These were usually triggered by bursts of energy that the owners were unable to quickly channel away from the other dogs. One or the other of the girls would come in from playing outside, bringing her exuberance with her. The other dog was typically calm and relaxed. When abruptly confronted with the sudden change in energy, the relaxing dog would take issue and sometimes retaliate.

For the most part, leadership was present in this dog/human relationship. The owners practiced many common sense activities with the dogs. "Protocol" exercises (Chapter 7) had been inconsistent, so some improvement was made there. The biggest issue was, for Shady, lack of constructive exercise. Owing to her "embarrassing" outbursts, the owners grew

less and less enthusiastic about the walks. They were, for them, simply draining. And so, the problem got worse.

The owners tried many different types of corrections, but, because of this dog's predisposition to being hard-headed and oblivious to pain, it only seemed to escalate her behavior. Attempts at desensitization, hoping she would eventually calm down, were also ineffective. That approach simply drew too much attention to the owners. Neighbors began staring disapprovingly as the owners stood for long periods, allowing Shady to "carry on".

Since Shady was already stressed due to insufficient exercise, adding more stress to the walks with constant corrections seemed to make it worse. Eventually, for this dog, the only approach that seemed to work was to completely distract her attention away from the other dog, using food as a lure. It allowed just enough time for the dog to refocus on the owner. The temporary use of food, in this situation, reconditioned the dog to see that walks could involve something beyond tension and anxiety. While the issue of *enough* exercise still needed to be addressed, at least this made it possible for the owners to make a commitment to get the dog out more often.

The Case of Rufus

A couple contacted me for training with an adopted dog from P.A.W.S. The dog in question was a neutered male, approx. 18 mo. old, German Shepherd/Huskie mix. Early on, the dog displayed aggression toward the husband, especially when any physical contact was made around the dog's scruff or neck area. He also made frequent aggressive displays during encounters with other dogs.

Some other facts surrounding this case were:

1. The dog was a confident, assertive personality type.
2. The dog had been "over-corrected" in the past, leading to his present mistrust of and defensive reaction to any corrections.
3. The dog had inadequate socialization, so his skill level in being able to modify his behavior was limited, especially with other dogs.

Trust was a major factor here, as it is in most cases of "mishandled" dogs. While corrections were not tossed out, they were kept in check, allowing the dog to learn that control should be exhibited not just by *him,* but also by the *leader.* As both dog and owners became more familiar and confident with each other, socialization progressed as well. Eventually, Rufus enjoyed interacting with a variety of dogs without incident. Over time, as he matured, the owners told me he became a most remarkable dog, rarely requiring much more than an occasional mild verbal reminder. Furthermore, the bond between Rufus and the husband (where originally it was rather tenuous) became incredibly solid.

• Intra-Sexual Aggression •

Within a pack, as dogs of the same gender mature and go through adolescence, the issue of same-gender

sparring is not uncommon. This usually occurs within the "Beta" group (see Chapter 1), that contains dogs with enough energy, intelligence and drive to have hopes of someday being the leader. Only certain dogs within the pack are allowed to breed. Those at the top will decide which dogs will be allowed to reproduce. This ensures that only the strongest, healthiest and most viable genes will be passed on.

When dogs reach the age of sexual maturity (beginning at about 5-6 months) hormonal changes within their bodies can trigger more contentious behavior. Intact males view other intact males as a potential threat and will often fight for rank position. The same can occur between females. The higher up one gets in the pecking order, the more likely one is to be a possible candidate for future leader. The occasional sparring that occurs between *opposite-*gendered dogs is typically not rank-oriented.

In households where rules are lax or even non-existent, dogs will invariably construct their own ranking systems, especially between like-gendered dogs. This is not to say that dogs of like-gender cannot co-exist peaceably. Where rules and structure *are* clearly delineated, dogs are far less likely to be contentious with each other. Therefore, the most important aspect to reducing intra-sexual aggression is to establish a solid social structure with *humans* as the leaders. Daily rituals and protocol exercises will also help the dogs focus on what is expected of them, gently but consistently reminding the dog of their rank.

Where there is no intention to use a dog for breeding, the owner should have the dog spayed or neutered. Not only does this greatly reduce the occurrence of hormonally triggered aggression, it is also better for the health of the dog. Dogs that are left intact but never bred have a much higher rate of cancer than their counterparts.

The Case of Blue and Eagle Bait

When I was contacted, this family had 5 Dachshunds: 3 males (all neutered) and 2 females (1 spayed). The violent aggressive outbursts had only begun in the last few months, with a tell-tale addition to the pack.

In the very beginning, a few years prior, this "pack" consisted of all spayed females, and only one male (Blue) who was intact. When the oldest female passed away, the couple eventually replaced her with a male Dachshund puppy. Another male and female puppy (both Dachshunds as well) were added over time, bringing the total to 5 — 3 males, 2 females. Blue, the oldest, was still intact (un-neutered) at this point. The last important fact regarding this case was that, throughout the dogs' lives, no formal training had been sought. Rules were generally lax, with just plenty of love and affection to go around.

The fights began when the first new pup, Eagle Bait, reached adolescence. At six months, there was now the very obvious ingredient of testosterone added to the mix. Blue, the oldest male, at 4½ years,

now viewed Eagle Bait as a threat to the control of the pack. As the fights escalated, both males were subsequently neutered. Unfortunately, the precedent had already been set, so it didn't really solve the problem.

Furthermore, the other equally important issue in this situation still remained unchanged: there was still no *leadership* coming from the owners. Rules continued to be vague or non-existent, the dogs being allowed to set the status quo amongst themselves.

This case demonstrates the intricacies of dog-to-dog communication, something that owners are often unaware of. Not understanding the drives and thought patterns of dog behavior and dog psychology can leave owners completely unprepared when aggression rears its ugly head. This case was months, if not years in the development, with the owners totally in the dark. All that was needed was the right catalyst—and that came with Eagle Bait. The factors at work in this case were:

1. no rules or expectations for the dogs,

2. insufficient *constructive* exercise,

3. more than one intact male coupled with the preceding factors. It was, quite simply, a ticking bomb.

As each of these items was addressed, the aggression and fighting between the males subsequently subsided. It did not disappear overnight, and did require solid vigilance from the owners, guiding and directing the dogs *and* the environment. However, in the end, all learned to live relatively peaceably together.

▪ Parental Aggression ▪

Like most of the other aggressive drives, this is also instinctive, based on the primal necessity of protecting the young. It is present in both genders, although more so with females. When a bitch has a litter of pups, always be cautious about approaching, *especially* if you are unfamiliar with the dog. If she shows any signs of concern or anxiety, it is best not to pursue the matter. I do not correct females for showing natural protective behavior for their babies. With these types of situations, it is best to simply be one step ahead of the dog, planning ahead and controlling the environment before the dog feels a need to react.

The Case of Lily and Her Pups

When my oldest bitch, Lily, had her first litter, we all had a lot to learn. She was an excellent mother, very attentive and fastidious, but maybe a little overwhelmed with 10 babies. When the pups were old enough to start finding homes for them, she was allowed to be present when people came to look at them. She never showed any serious protective aggression, although she seemed to insist on being in attendance, observing, as the people interacted with her pups.

The second litter was completely different. At 4 years old, her maturity and previous experience gave her a little more of a wary edge to her behavior with strangers. She displayed definite apprehension when people walked up to the puppy pen. I knew she would not have allowed anyone to come inside

and pick up one of her babies—even with me standing there. I decided it would simply be easier to remove her to another area before potential purchasers came over.

• Possessive Aggression •

In this type of aggression, we see *guarding* behaviors. It is generally observed with an object, something the dog sees as valuable at a particular moment in time. Depending on the rank of the dog in question, how intensely she wants the item, and the rank of the dog that is challenging her, she will either guard the object fiercely or half-heartedly. The controlling of "resources" is a fact of life, one that dogs are acutely aware of. While, on the whole, dogs are willing to compromise most issues, humans nevertheless see displays of an unwillingness to share *all* things at *all* times. It can be a display over a favorite toy, a choice bone, a favorite sleeping spot, or a human being.

This type of aggression also hinges to a degree on Personal Space. The more favored the object, the more a particular dog may extend her "space" surrounding her. For instance, if it's a brand new, meaty bone, the growling may begin when a "challenger" is still many feet away, let alone getting close enough to touch the dog. I observe this frequently at my house with my own dogs. While there are usually enough bones to go around, more often than not, my youngest female (a very sassy, vivacious personality) will horde these resources, refusing to share with the other dogs. She may allow them to come quite close, but she's ready with a quick snap if they try to take one. *I, however,* can, at any time, walk right up to the dog and remove any or all the bones from her without incident. That is afforded me due to my rank as leader.

While I am acutely aware of the risks in standing up to a dog who is growling at you over something he wants, setting a precedent that lets the dog remain in control is not recommended. Pack leaders are ultimately in charge of and claim possession to *all* resources. An attitude that allows for "it's the dog's, so don't challenge him" can too easily spill over into other areas. If the dog feels she can get away with controlling the owner/environment in one way, it's not unlikely she will try her hand with other "resources" as well.

Be very cautious in situations where it appears the dog is guarding *people.* There is a profound difference between a dog who shows natural protective behavior for pack members, and one who is acting like he *owns* a particular person (read the case of Lennox below). While it may seem to be an asset, for instance, to have a dog that "protects the baby" (as some of my students have told me) how likely are owners to defend the dog's behavior if Grandma gets bitten when she comes to visit the little tyke?

Food guarding aggression, in particular, is instinctual in the wild. One dog will naturally want to hold onto his portion. With domestic dogs, the vast majority of them quickly see that humans are not a

threat to their food portion. However, if your dog exhibits these behaviors, work on general desensitizing and protocol exercises to establish rank, as well as helping the dog to relax with the presence of people when he's eating. Don't do any "grandstanding" such as sticking your hand abruptly into his dish! Simply standing nearby while he's eating is a good start. Periodically walking up and *adding* something special or "extra" to his meal while he's eating can also get him to view your approach as welcome and even exciting.

For guarding of "things", i.e. a bed or toy, protocol exercises can also be helpful. Play deliberately with the toy in the dog's presence, not allowing her to take it from you. Sit on her bed occasionally, placing the dog a few feet away in a "Sit/Stay". If there is any real concern about being bitten, *leave the leash on the dog*, so you can have control without having to get your hand right next to the dog. If you see what you consider extreme behavior in this area, seek professional assistance.

The Case of Maya

This was a 4-month old black Labrador Retriever, female. She had an average energy level for a pup her age, was moderately assertive, and essentially showed no abnormalities with her behavior, When Maya received her first edible bone, she was thrilled. Settling down immediately with it, she began to make short work of it, eating nearly half of it within a few minutes. When one of the family's young boys walked up to the dog, she growled threateningly. He backed off in surprise and fear. This was brought to my attention at the next lesson. We practiced a "Give and Take" exercise:

- Put the dog in a "Sit/Stay" with the leash on.
- Offer the bone.
- Pause 2-3 seconds.
- Gently, take the bone away. (Hold the leash if needed.)
- Praise the dog.
- Pause 2-3 seconds.
- Give the bone back to the dog.

Follow this sequence 6-8 times in a row, keeping it calm and non-threatening. Another good exercise is to *hold the bone* in your hand while the dog chews on it. This may not always be feasible, but will also demonstrate to the dog that you are not *threatening* her.

The Case of Lennox

A young couple, expecting their first child, called me in due to aggressive displays toward the husband from their 1 year old neutered male Saint Bernard, Lennox. According to the husband, the dog had seemed to become progressively more protective of his wife since she had become pregnant. Lennox had even gone so far as to bite the husband when he tried to show affection to his wife. With just a few questions, it became obvious that Lennox was quite spoiled and pampered. He slept wherever he chose to, had near constant affection lavished on him, was served grilled salmon, pot roast and leftover meat loaf. He did receive fairly regular exercise, but was not held to any firm, consistent or tangible

rules. In a sense, *Lennox* had made the rules, and the owners obeyed. The specific behavior towards the husband wasn't so much "protecting the wife" as it was "keeping the husband away". In Lennox's mind, he had claimed the wife as a "resource". This was, of course, quite a shock to the husband.

The solution to this dilemma was, actually, quite simple. The owners had only to begin standing firm with their *passive messages*. Lennox was no longer allowed onto the bed or furniture. A leash was left on him to facilitate following through with the new rules. Mealtimes became very routine, amounting to a bowl of kibbles, with Lennox being made to Sit and wait before eating. Physical affection was dramatically cut back, and offered only when "earned". Exercise was increased and, in general, involved much more structure than before. Guests that came over were informed of the new rules, and asked to participate and reinforce the new expectations for the dog. Within less than a month, Lennox was a changed dog, much to the delight of the couple.

• Predatory Aggression •

This, like many of the other types of aggression, is also instinctive. It is the hunt drive, seen in the dog's tendency to pursue objects or animals that dart rapidly past. Some breeds have had this characteristic deliberately accentuated, as in herding breeds. However, the culmination of the "hunt", which is to kill the prey, has been largely controlled. Most dogs will react to rapidly moving visual stimulation. It could be a squirrel, a cat, another dog, a bicyclist, a car or a running child. I've even encountered dogs who became fixated on a spot of refracted light from a prism in the window.

This behavior can be triggered all too easily where there is inadequate training and socialization. Dogs with insufficient exercise can also be prone to overreactions to sudden visual stimulation. Young children playing around dogs can be particularly vulnerable to this type of aggressive display. Supervision in these types of situations is *strongly encouraged*, especially with puppies and/or dogs with excitable temperaments. In many cases, exercises that desensitize the dog to the stimuli are effective. I will often use a ball as a distraction during a Sit/Stay, tossing it back and forth past the dog. I also encourage students to practice with their dogs in or near areas with children (schoolyards excepted, due to regulations).

The Case of Lady and the Cat

A family left their 15-month old female German Shepherd, Lady, with me for dog sitting. These people were, as a rule, not cat lovers, and whenever one happened to jump on their fence at home, or enter their yard, they encouraged the dog to chase it out. Over time, the dog grew into a true "cat hunter", always on alert and generally over-reacting to them whenever she saw them. I explained to them the liabilities of over-exciting the prey drive, but that did not prevent the incident that occurred at my house.

I have always had cats as well as dogs in my house. Being aware of Lady's predilection for felines, I was

cautious every time our cat entered the room with her. One day, though, I was unaware the cat was across the room behind me. Lady abruptly pushed past me and, before I could grab her, took off after the cat, in serious and deadly pursuit. As she rounded the corner and headed for the stairs, I was able to meet her from the other direction. When she tried to dart past me, the only thing left to grab was her tail. (I was thankful she wasn't an *Australian Shepherd*—no tail) It successfully stopped the pursuit. It was obvious from her intensity, that *play* was not what Lady had on her mind.

Predatory aggression is not a game, and to encourage it in a dog can easily turn ugly in the wrong situation. The dog does not have the ability to discriminate one prey from another. That task should fall to the owners.

The Case of Maggie and the "Pickle" Ball

Maggie was a 3-year old female German Pointer. Her temperament was decidedly excitable, as is typical with most bird dogs. In general, she did well with training and responded easily to the leadership of the owners. However, her instinctive breeding to pursue fast moving objects proved to be an issue when her owners wanted to play "Pickle" ball. This is a game similar to squash or tennis. The owners, in fact, had a "Pickle" ball court on their property. They found it completely impossible to play the game unless Maggie was put into the house, and then she would often bark and carry-on out of frustration. If she was allowed outside, she would invariably leap at the ball and run off with it.

Desensitizing exercises worked best for this dog. One or the other of the couple would enforce the Sit/Stay with the leash on, while the other would paddle the ball around for a few minutes at a time. Maggie did eventually respond to this — though it took some time. Her breeding and instinct tended to revolt at this. On an *individual* level for German Pointers, she was on the high end for energy level, so results were slow in coming.

While it may be hard to see how "aggression" is part of chasing a ball, to the dog, it is simply seen as "prey". Dogs do not discriminate between animate or inanimate. Had the ball been replaced with a squirrel, for instance, the dog would have taken the behavior to another level, likely killing the animal once she had caught it.

■ Territorial Aggression ■

This is an instinctive behavior with most dogs — a drive to defend "turf" that belongs to the pack. In the wild, it is driven by a need to preserve the food resources in an area to ensure the survival of the group. With domestic dogs, this behavior is readily observed any given day of the week, walking past neighbors' yards. Dogs will run the fence line, barking frantically. Some displays are quite intimidating. Conversely, most of these dogs would probably behave quite differently in a neutral area, away from their homes. Their drive to defend territory was left behind when they walked off the property.

According to Karen Delise in her book *Fatal Dog Attacks*, the issue of territorial aggression ranks as the most prominent factor leading to fatal encounters with dogs. In data collected from 1965-2001, over 50% of fatal attacks against humans involved dogs who were either chained, loose in a yard, or confined in a kennel. Humans underestimate the intensity of this drive in many situations. Dogs who are chained perpetually in back yards operate on a much higher level of frustration. "Because dogs are territorial animals, chaining them only serves to exacerbate space issues, as space is limited and more clearly defined... The dog is cognizant of the fact that he can only retreat the length of the chain and will often opt to 'stand his ground'. Removing the option of flight for any animal will always increase the chance of a physical encounter (or fight response) to a perceived threat."[3]

Almost every dog will react instinctively to a perceived threat or intruder to their territory, whether that is the backyard, the house or a car. This reaction will almost always begin with an alert bark, and then escalate depending on the dog and/or the situation. The problem doesn't lie with the dog just *barking*. The problem is with dogs who don't know when to "turn it off" once their owner has arrived and/or determined that there is no longer a threat. Again, this goes back to the dog learning to accept and follow the larger decision of the owner during a stressful situation.

3. *Fatal Dog Attacks, The Stories Behind the Statistics.* Karen Delise. Anubis Press, Manorville, New York. 2002.

When encountering a dog who is displaying territorial aggression, one of the worst mistakes a human can make is to continue forward, encroaching farther into the dog's space. Inadvertently making direct eye contact with the dog can also bode ill for the human, as the dog will likely take this as a challenge. If you find yourself suddenly challenged by a dog on his turf, the best suggestion is to *psychologically* defer to the dog as much as possible in an attempt to defuse the energy. Even if you know the dog, it is not recommended that you use this situation to "get friendly". Also, operating on the assumption that the dog will *only* bark at you is risky at best. Fold your arms across your chest, stand perfectly still and drop your gaze away from the dog. Under *no circumstances* should you try to "scare" the dog off by shouting or waving your arms. Make absolutely no sudden movements. ***Do Not Run!*** Wait and allow the dog to see that you are not a threat. In *most* cases, the dog will gradually move off if you "defer" to him. At this point, *slowly* retreat in a side-wise manner, keeping the dog in your peripheral view. If he decides to approach a second time, go through the above suggestions again.

The Case of Woody and the Utility Man

Years ago, I owned a large male Doberman Pinscher. While he was very well-trained and socialized (especially with children) Woody took his back yard guard duty very seriously. He was alert and "on patrol" when in the backyard, even more so when he knew no on was at home.

On one particular afternoon, I had been doing yard work, passing in and out of the yard through the side gate. Consequently, it was not locked when this incident occurred. The meter reader for the utility company was making his rounds. When he got to our house, he walked boldly into the back yard, completely ignoring the prominently mounted "Beware of Dog" sign on the fence. Hearing the commotion, I came running around the side of the house. By then, Woody had cornered the meter reader against the wall, his clipboard held out as a barricade between himself and the dog. In his protection training, Woody was specifically taught to "hold" the subject. I called the dog off immediately, no one was bitten. In future, the electric company sent us the forms and we filled out the cards ourselves.

This case is different than most in that Woody had had formal training to do what he did that afternoon. While many dogs would likely have challenged the meter reader in some fashion, the chances of his getting bitten would depend on the confidence level of the dog. A timid, fearful dog might have tried to bite the man as he was leaving. A more assertive dog might never have allowed the utility man into the yard. If you have a dog that shows moderate to high levels of territorial behavior, post signs prominently, including purchasing a lock for the gate. The law is very clear in most states on dog bites—not particularly in favor of the dog or dog owner, especially where negligence can be shown.

The Case of Pyro, the Russian Laika

In this case, I was contacted because the dog was lifting his leg inside the house—specifically in the front living room, on the corner of the sofa. This behavior occurred nowhere else in the house. Upon arriving at the family's home, I saw that the living room window afforded a full view of the front yard as well as the sidewalk that went by the house. While sitting in the front room with the family, I saw a neighbor walk by with their dog, allowing him to lift his left on the shrub in the family's front yard. Also observing this was Pyro, who became greatly agitated, running back and forth, jumping and barking at the window, trying to get out to this other dog. When his attempts were met with frustration, he promptly went over and lifted his leg on the corner of the sofa.

When questioned, the owners told me that they consistently allowed Pyro to lift his leg and mark territory whenever and wherever he pleased when he was out for a walk. In essence, Pyro, an assertive, confident male dog, had been encouraged to extend his territory all over the neighborhood. When he saw what amounted to an "intruder" on his territory, he instinctively felt a need to "patrol" and defend said "territory". However, he was thwarted in this drive by the front window. As a frustration response, he opted to mark out his turf in the living room.

The solution for these people was two-fold:

1. Pyro was no longer allowed to urinate on walks, and

2. the curtains in the living room were closed when Pyro was in the house, preventing him from seeing what was happening in the front yard.

Territorial aggression is not something an owner should need or want to totally squash. In fact, in the majority of cases, owners admit they feel safer knowing their dog will alert them to odd or unfamiliar noises. The problem lies in how the initial "alert" phase can escalate into a potential attack. It then becomes a legal matter, especially if a person gets bitten or mauled.

Learning to channel and control territorial aggression is extremely important. When training for obedience, the dog should learn to accept the decisions of the leader--that's *you*. Making sure the dog has reasonable social confidence will also help to reduce the intensity and duration of the dog's stress reaction. A dog who cannot or will not turn to the owner for direction is ***not*** an asset. It is only a liability. If you feel you cannot adequately handle a situation that involves aggression, ***please*** seek professional assistance. With the right guidance, many, if not most, cases can be improved. Some can even be completely cured.

CONCLUSION

▪ THE TAIL END ▪

Photo courtesy Bennett & Hastings

A few last remarks seem appropriate to draw things together. Training dogs and people is anything but perfect and exact. There are more combinations of environments, distractions, moods, instinctive drives and personalities than any one person can possibly be prepared for. I do not say this to discourage training your dog—if that were the case, I wouldn't have written this book. Rather, I wish to acknowledge that, however one may strive for perfection as the goal, it will never be *completely* achieved unless we were to become dogs ourselves. Because we are *human*, we are limited within our human sphere. Because the dog is what he is, he is limited within his dog sphere.

Acknowledging that mistakes happen will keep the relationship realistic. I would be suspicious of any person or trainer who claimed to have a "perfect" dog. One trainer, while demonstrating his dog's skill at Protection Training, was unable to call his dog "Off" on command. Another trainer I knew was unable to Recall his dog when he unhooked the leash—the dog ran playfully across the field. I've seen service dogs veer distractedly toward other animals. By all accounts, each and every one of these dogs was very "well-trained". In addition, the training methods used were as varied as the dogs, hence one could not necessarily blame the methodology.

My own dogs are not perfect. I work within a 5% or less margin of error, and the dogs usually give me that. It takes hard work, persistence and an open mind. I will always be learning about my dogs and the work of training and communicating with them is always a work in progress. I know they are worth it.

RECOMMENDED READING

▪ GENERAL READING/DOG PSYCHOLOGY ▪

Boone, Allen J. Kinship With All Life. San Francisco, Harper. 1954.

Chartwell Books. The Giant Book of the Dog. 1998.

Donaldson, Jean. The Culture Clash. Berkley, Calif. James and Kenneth Publishers. 2005.

Fogle, Bruce, D.V.M., M.R.C.V.S. The Dog's Mind, Understanding Your Dog's Behavior. New York, Howell Book House. 1990.

Fox, Dr. Michael W. Understanding Your Dog. New York, St. Martin's Griffin. 1972.

Lorenz, Konrad. Man Meets Dog. New York, Kodansha International. 1953.

McConnell, Patricia B., Ph. D. The Other End Of The Leash. New York, Ballantine Books. 2002.

Milani, Myrna, D.V.M. The Body Language and Emotions of Dogs. New York, Quill William Morrow. 1986.

McLoughlin, John C. The Canine Clan, A New Look at Man's Best Friend. New York, Viking Press. 1983.

Monks of New Skete. How To Be Your Dog's Best Friend. New York, Little, Brown Publishers. 2002.

Thomas, Elizabeth Marshall. The Hidden Life of Dogs. Boston, Houghton Mifflin. 1993.

Whitney, Leon F. D.V.M. <u>Dog Psychology, The Basis of Dog Training</u>. New York, Howell Book House. 1984

▪ Dog Language/Communication ▪

Abrantes, Roger. <u>Dog Language, An Encyclopedia of Canine Behaviour.</u> Wakan Tanka Publishers. 1997.

Aloff, Brenda. <u>Canine Body Language, A Photographic Guide.</u> DogWise Publishers. 2005.

Fogle, Bruce, D.V.M. <u>If Your Dog Could Talk.</u> Dorling Kindersley. 1992.

Rugaas, Turid. <u>On Talking Terms With Dogs, Calming Signals</u>. Hawaii, Legacy by Mail, Inc., 1997.

▪ Behavior Problems ▪

Aloff, Brenda. <u>Aggression In Dogs, Practical Management, Prevention & Behaviour Modification.</u> DogWise Publishers. 2002.

Benjamin, Carol Lea. <u>Dog Problems.</u> New York, Doubleday. 1981.

Campbell, William E. <u>Behavior Problems in Dogs.</u> American Veterinary Publications, Inc. 1975.

Dodman, Nicholas. <u>Dogs Behaving Badly</u>. New York. Bantam. 2000.

Donaldson, Jean. <u>Dogs Are From Neptune.</u> Lasar Multimedia Productions Inc. 1998.

▪ PUPPY CARE ▪

Lee, Muriel P. The Whelping and Rearing of Puppies, A Complete and Practical Guide.
T.F.H. Publications. 1997.
Monks of New Skete, The Art of Raising a Puppy.
Boston. Little, Brown. 1991.
Rutherford, Clarice, and David H. Neil. How to Raise A Puppy You Can Live With. Loveland, CO. Alpine Publications. 1981.

▪ OBEDIENCE TRAINING ▪

Benjamin, Carol Lea. Mother Knows Best. New York. Howell, 1987
Campbell, William. Owner's Guide to Better Behavior in Dogs. Loveland, CO. Blue Ribbon Books. 1995.
Frost, April. Beyond Obedience. New York. Three Rivers Press, 1998.
Koehler, William. The Koehler Method of Dog Training. New York. Howell, 1969.
Most, Konrad. Training Dogs. London. Popular Dogs, 1974.
Pryor, Karen. Don't Shoot the Dog. New York. Bantam, 1985.
Volhard, Joachim and Gail Tarmases Fisher. Training Your Dog. New York. Howell, 1983.
Woodhouse, Barbara. No Bad Dogs. New York. Summit Books, 1982.

GLOSSARY

Alpha: within a wolf or dog pack, the leaders or highest ranking members.

Allelomimetic: contagious behavior. Often marked by imitative behavior, such as group howling or "alert" reactions to a perceived threat.

Anthropomorphize: to attribute human form, characteristics or traits to a non-human or animal entity.

Aversive: in training, the use of a negative reinforcer or response, to reduce the occurrence of a specific behavior.

Beta: within a wolf or dog pack, the group ranking directly below the alphas or leaders.

Conspecific: within a wolf or dog pack, refers to fellow pack members, primarily but not limited to those of equal rank.

Drive: a purposeful energy, force, urge or basic need.

Discipline: control or order exerted over people or animals. A system or rules used to maintain such control. Bring under control by training in obedience.

Ethologist: one who studies the science of dog behavior.

Event Marker: in training, a deliberate action, sound or response that immediately marks a specific behavior for the dog as "good" or "bad".

Micturition: urination for the purpose of scent marking, establishment of territorial boundaries.

Operant Conditioning: a method of training based on "operants"--an item, behavior or response that effects or changes behavior or the environment. Reinforcers, either positive or negative, are "operants".

Reward: in training, a pleasant experience or consequence that the dog receives after having performed a specific behavior. Usually considered a positive reinforcer.

Spontaneous Recovery: in training, the sudden recurrence of a behavior that was thought to be "extinct". Usually triggered by environmental stimuli.

INDEX

2568838

Made in the USA